# Regulating Financial Markets

# Regulating Financial Markets

## A Critique and Some Proposals

George J. Benston

The AEI Press

*Publisher for the American Enterprise Institute*
WASHINGTON, D.C.

*1999*

Distributed to the Trade by National Book Network, 15200 NBN Way, Blue Ridge Summit, PA 17214. To order call toll free 1-800-462-6420 or 1-717-794-3800. For all other inquiries please contact the AEI Press, 1150 Seventeenth Street, N.W., Washington, D.C. 20036 or call 1-800-862-5801.

**Library of Congress Cataloging-in-Publication Data**

Benston, George J.
    Regulating financial markets : a critique and some proposals /
George J. Benston.
      p.  cm.
    Includes bibliographical references and index.
    ISBN 0-8447-4124-8 (paperback : alk. paper)
    1. Financial services industry—Law and legislation.  2. Banking
law.  I. Title.
    K1066.B46  1999
    346'.082—dc21                                    99-35733
                                                         CIP

ISBN 978-0-8447-4124-6

The Institute of Economic Affairs (London, UK) published a version of this study in 1998 as Hobart Paper 135.

THE AEI PRESS
Publisher for the American Enterprise Institute
1150 Seventeenth Street, N.W.
Washington, D.C. 20036

# ⌘

# *Contents*

# ⌘

# *Preface*

This study had its origins in a suggestion by Professor Geoffrey Wood of City University, London. Several years ago, he urged me to bring together all the work on banking, securities markets, and regulation that I had published since my graduation from the University of Chicago in 1962. I started to do this, but new research projects kept attracting my attention and absorbing all available time. Finally, when he bestowed on me the honor of presenting the nineteenth Henry Thornton Lecture at City University in November 1997, I took the opportunity to summarize my thinking, by then expanded to include government regulation of all financial services. For this opportunity, for many years of good conversations and occasional arguments, and for helpful comments on this monograph, I thank Geoffrey Wood. Professors George Kaufman (Loyola University, Chicago), David Blackwell (Emory University), David Llewellyn (Loughborough University), Harold Rose (London Business School), Mark Flannery (University of Florida), and Larry Wall (Federal Reserve Bank of Atlanta) also made very helpful comments and suggestions, for which I am most grateful.

My own work is overwhelmingly referenced in the manuscript for two reasons. First, this is a compilation of my research and ideas that have developed over the past thirty-five years. Second, to keep the manuscript to a reasonable size, I have not included the research findings and references to other ideas that appear in my papers. Readers can find support for the conclusions expressed here in those works.

# 1

## Introduction and Overview

Financial services, firms that provide these services, and financial markets are regulated worldwide to a greater extent than are most other products and services, with the exception of those that affect people's health and safety. Why is this? Indeed, why were financial firms and services regulated by governments long before they became concerned with their citizens' health and safety, or even with their economic well-being? What is the current justification for these regulations? Should financial services be regulated at all? If they should be regulated, which regulations would serve public purposes best and which would be harmful?

These questions are considered and answered in four chapters. The first sets the stage for the inquiry with a brief summary of the government regulations that are imposed on financial services. An overview of the balance of the study is then presented. Chapter 2 delineates and analyzes the reasons and justifications for regulation. Chapter 3 presents the costs of regulation, and chapter 4 proposes a reformed regulatory system.

The public choice about whether and to what extent financial services, firms, and markets should be regulated is not a choice between a perfect regulator who acts to secure the public good and perfect markets that can only be worsened by regulation. Both regulator and markets are staffed and managed by people who act to maximize and secure their own welfare, subject to such various constraints as ability, tastes, ethics, and costs imposed by others. Consequently, both are imperfect. Some regulations would benefit the general public if they were well administered, but because the general public consists of many people with different interests, these regulations might be administered to benefit some people at the expense of others. Other regulations have been established purposely to benefit specific people, often at the expense of others. Some producers of financial products seek to produce good products that are fairly priced; others hope to get by with whatever they can, at as high a price as they can charge.

This monograph distinguishes those situations where regulation is likely to be helpful from those where it is likely to be harmful. In general, economic reasoning tested with empirical studies leads me to conclude that some regulation of financial-services providers is desirable—namely, capital requirements of depositories and some insurance companies—but not much more. First, I will examine the origins of government regulation of financial services to determine whether the removal of these regulations might restore the problems that regulations are supposed to have solved.

## Governmental Regulation of Financial Services

Financial services have been regulated by governments, in one way or another, for centuries.[1] Regulation of financial-services providers has taken the form of restrictions on entry; of controls over the products that could be offered and the assets that could and must be held; and of restraints on the prices that could be paid or received. Financial institutions have had to prepare and submit financial and other reports of their conditions and operations, both to the general public and to regulatory agencies, for which the form and the contents have been specified. The reports have been subject to examination and review by government agents. The amount of capital (equity and sometimes subordinated debt) that must be contributed and maintained has often been specified.

Participants in financial markets and the terms of products offered in those markets have also been subject to regulation. Insurance agents and brokers have had to obtain licenses, and in some countries limits have been placed on the financial products that could be sold. These regulations have been extended internationally to the operations of domestic firms operating in other countries and to foreign firms operating in domestic markets. National regulators of financial products have attempted to coordinate their activities with those of comparable regulators in other countries and to harmonize their rules.

In most countries entry has been restricted at one time or another. Banks could not offer financial services to the public unless they were chartered or licensed. Furthermore, the charters were and are difficult and often costly to acquire, relative to the licenses required for other businesses. The possible exceptions to this generality are businesses that offer products that, at times, have offended public morality, such as liquor, gambling, and prostitution. In some states of the United States, banks were forbidden to open branches or their branching operations were restricted to geographical subunits, such as cities and counties. Until the 1990s, the United States, alone among countries, prohibited nationwide (interstate) branching, with a few exceptions. Firms that underwrite and sell insurance often must be licensed, and firms that offer securities services to the public must be registered with regulatory agencies. Firms that underwrite securities, though, rarely must be specially licensed or regulated directly. Their sales personnel, however, usually must be licensed.

The products that financial institutions could offer to the public have also been restricted. Although several countries, notably Germany, have for well over a century allowed banks to offer a wide range of financial services, the United States and other countries have severely restricted their banks' activities. Since 1933, the Glass-Steagall Act has forbidden commercial banks from domestically underwriting and trading all but federal-government and some state and municipal obligations, although they can underwrite and trade securities in most other countries. Increasingly liberal interpretations of the act by bank regulators, though, have reduced the domestic restrictions. Banks now can be associated with discount-brokerage firms and, with some restrictions, with full-service securities firms.

But neither U.S. banks nor their holding companies can own an insurance company. Further, the United States and most other countries have permitted only commercial banks to offer demand-deposit services, although in the past several decades in the United States this privilege was extended to savings and loan associations and credit unions. It is likely that these institutions were allowed to provide this essential banking service because they had previously circumvented the restrictions by defining checks as negotiable orders of withdrawal (NOW) from savings accounts and as drafts on share accounts (share drafts). Securities firms are not permitted to offer demand deposits, although they have done so effectively by permitting holders of their money market funds to make withdrawals with checks drawn through banks.

Commercial banks in the United States are not permitted to invest in equity securities, although banks chartered by some states and savings and loan associations can do so to a limited extent. Nor can real estate be owned except as required for operations—which are often defined to include a large building, most of which is rented out. Banks and insurance companies are generally permitted to hold only "investment grade" securities. Depositories in the United States and some other countries must hold a specified fraction of their deposits in a non-interest-bearing account with the central bank (or in vault cash), while insurance companies must maintain asset reserves sufficient to pay policyholders' claims.

Interest paid and charged by financial institutions for deposits and loans has been restricted. Deposit-interest rates have been regulated in many countries. Interest-rate (usury) ceilings on loans have also been imposed on lenders generally, although the United Kingdom largely abolished these restrictions in the eighteenth century. The United States has at times imposed maturity restrictions on consumer loans, and has specified the collateral requirements for loans used to purchase securities. Premiums on property and casualty (accident) insurance—but not on life and health insurance—have been subjected to both minimum and maximum schedules by state insurance commissioners in the United States.

Owners of banks, insurance companies, and securities firms are required to invest and maintain a minimum amount of equity capital. The percentages have at times been tied to the presumed risk of the institutions' assets. To a limited extent, debt capital that is subordinated to other liabilities may meet capital requirements.

Government officials have subjected financial institutions and insurance companies to detailed supervision and examination. In most countries, financial institutions must periodically render reports of their financial conditions and operations to a government agency. An early requirement imposed on depository institutions has been the publication of statements of financial condition. In the United States, banks' and insurance companies' financial records and operations are subject to field examinations. Many other countries rely on independent accountants to audit banks' and insurance companies' financial reports. If the institutions fail to comply with regulatory requirements, the regulatory agency can force compliance through court orders. In extreme situations, and when the institutions are considered to be insolvent, their charters may be revoked.

In the United States, particularly, "unfair" (invidious) discrimination against such people as African Americans, Hispanics and other minorities, foreign-born persons, and females has been generally prohibited. But chartered depositories (banks and savings and loan associations), almost uniquely, are periodically examined to determine whether they have practiced such discrimination. These compliance examinations are conducted annually, and banks' customers are encouraged to complain to the authorities if they believe they have been mistreated.

As commerce has become increasingly international, so has the regulation of financial institutions. A uniform capital requirement for international banks (the Basel Agreement) has been devised and adopted by those developed countries with the largest economies, most of which have adopted this standard for all their banks. Uniform capital standards have been proposed for securities firms as well. International cooperation by banking and securities regulators has been attempted, and harmonization of domestic regulations has been urged.

The markets for financial services have also been regulated. As noted earlier, securities trading may be offered only by licensed brokers, and insurance only by licensed salespersons and agencies. The way that financial products are structured is often subject to government approval. The minimum information that purchasers of financial products must be given has been prescribed. Extensive regulation is imposed on the financial statements provided by corporations wishing to sell their equities and debt to the public. In the United Kingdom, requirements imposed by the Companies Acts have been general in nature. In the United States, securities acts legislated in 1933 and 1934 regulate the specific contents of prospectuses and periodic financial statements. In recent years, other countries have moved toward the U.S. approach.

Although other businesses and products have also been subjected to governmental regulation, banks were regulated earlier and more extensively than any other kind of enterprise—even those producing goods and services that affect people's health and safety. Regulation of nonfinancial firms and of products generally was imposed much later, when consumer protection became a legislative goal. Unlike such products as food, heating, electricity, and transportation, however, financial services have little direct effect on people's health and safety. Although financial products affect people's economic well-being, so do vehicular and home repairs, along with many other products and services that are not subject to much regulation. What, then, is special about banks, securities firms, insurance companies, and financial services in general?

## Overview of the Balance of the Study

Chapter 2 delineates five basic reasons and justifications for regulating financial services. These are (1) benefits to government; (2) concern about negative externalities (for example, financial panics); (3) consumer protection; (4) appeal to popularly elected legislators; and (5) benefits to regulated financial institutions. Of these, I find that regulation is justified from the viewpoint of consumers only to reduce the negative externalities deriving from two sources: first, from the failure of insurance companies that provide government-mandated protection of noncontracting third parties, such as automobile liability insurance, and second, from taxpayers' and prudently run banks' having to "bail out" failed-banks' depositors. Although consumer protection can be a valid justification for regulation, there is no reason for regulating financial institutions or products *more* than other firms or products—indeed, it is arguable that they should be *less* regulated.

(The solvency of companies that provide long-term insurance is a possible exception that can be dealt with efficiently.) The reasons for government regulation are found in the first, fourth, and fifth items listed above. Regulation has provided and continues to provide benefits to governments, legislators, and regulated financial institutions. That is the principal reason why financial-services regulation was enacted and is sustained, although it is generally detrimental to most consumers.

*Benefits to government.* The benefits-to-government reason explains why banks were regulated earlier than almost any other enterprise. Regulation—primarily restriction of entry—was imposed so that governments and those they favored could benefit from the production of money and from the direct and indirect taxation of banks. Bank regulation continues in many countries as a means for government officials to channel funds to favored enterprises, projects, and persons.

*Concern about negative externalities.* Reason two, the concern about negative externalities, is the principal contemporary justification for regulation. In general, this concern provides an economically valid justification for governmental regulation—that is, if there really is an externality, and if the costs of regulation do not exceed the benefits from reducing it. Consequently, a substantial portion of chapter 2 is devoted to this justification for regulation. I describe and analyze six possible or alleged sources of negative externalities. Four of the six are concerned with the effects of the failure of financial institutions on the following: (1) noncontracting third parties, (2) other solvent institutions, (3) the payments system and securities markets, and (4) taxpayers and prudently run institutions that might have to bail out depositors of insolvent banks or beneficiaries of insurance companies. The other two possible negative externalities are (5) the unnecessarily high costs imposed on consumers because of their concerns about the solvency of financial institutions and the trustworthiness of financial instruments and (6) negative spillover effects on consumers and businesses in markets served by poorly performing financial institutions.

With respect to the first externality, only the failure of an insurance company that provides government-mandated insurance (for instance, on vehicles) would impose costs on noncontracting third parties (such as victims of an automobile accident). This is a negative externality that government regulation of insurance companies might mitigate. The second externality, negative effects on solvent institutions, does not actually give rise to negative consequences. On the contrary, the failure of a poorly or imprudently managed institution rewards prudently run institutions, as people concerned about solvency shift their business to companies that they believe will not fail.

The third possible externality is cited most often as a justification for regulating banks and other depositories: the failure of these institutions might result in runs on solvent institutions, and possibly in a very costly collapse of the financial system. Analysis reveals that this is not a problem for which regulation is required or necessary, principally for three reasons. First, this concern is meaningful only for depository institutions, because only runs on fractional-reserve depository institutions can destabilize the financial system. The failures of securities firms or insurance companies do not result in such systemically destabilizing runs, but rather in shifts of resources to firms that are perceived to be strong. Thus, prudent managers tend to be rewarded and markets tend to be stabilized. Second, runs on depository institutions have been rare and are virtually nonexistent when depositors are protected by deposit insurance. Large deposits, which might not be covered by insurance, would almost never be kept in cash; rather, withdrawn funds would be redeposited in banks perceived to be safe. Thus, even though banks might fail, the nation's total money supply and credit would be largely unchanged. And third, runs to currency, if they did occur, could be offset effectively by central bank purchases of assets (open-market operations). Consequently, concern about destabilizing runs is not a valid justification for regulating financial institutions or markets.

The fourth possible negative externality, the cost to taxpayers and to prudently managed financial institutions (which pay the cost of bailing out insolvent firms' depositors and insurance-policy beneficiaries), indeed does give rise to a cost that could justify some degree of governmental regulation. This eventuality is predicated on the validity of two assumptions. One is that such bailouts cannot be avoided politically—which experience shows is the case. The other assumption is that the regulation is efficient and not detrimental to competition—which would be the case if the system outlined in chapter 4 were adopted.

The fifth possible externality is positive: efficiently alleviating consumers' concerns about the solvency of financial institutions and the trustworthiness of financial instruments. The regulations that are expected to achieve this benefit usually take the form of governmental examination and supervision of banks and insurance companies, government-mandated and -dictated disclosure of financial statements, and governmental specification of the terms of financial instruments. Consumers would indeed benefit if they could be certain that their funds were not at risk of loss, and if they had access to useful information about companies in which they might invest and financial products that they might purchase. There could be a negative externality if, absent such governmental regulation, consumers would have to incur greater costs and, hence, to use fewer financial services than are optimal for the economy. The costs of regulation, though, are necessarily borne by consumers, and it is unlikely that government agents could know completely or adequately what information consumers require.

Nonetheless, producers of financial products have strong incentives to provide information that consumers might want. While some producers might not want to provide consumers with information, their competitors who offer superior products would benefit from informing those firms' customers. (Fraud and misrepresentation are considered later.) Consequently, I conclude that the costs of this seemingly reasonable justification for regulation would most likely exceed its benefits. Moreover, by imposing meaningful capital requirements, the government can efficiently assure consumers that banks and insurance companies are unlikely to become insolvent.

With respect to the final possible externality that might justify governmental regulation, the poor performance of financial institutions in serving their market areas could have spillover effects. This has been a concern in the United States under the general rubric of *redlining*—the presumed refusal of banks to offer mortgages and other loans, or of insurance companies to sell insurance, to people in "undesirable" areas, or to do so only on onerous terms. Another charge levied against some U.S. banks is that they discriminate invidiously against minorities, particularly African Americans. In other countries, it has been alleged that dominant financial institutions have not treated poor consumers and new business enterprises well. But evidence supporting these allegations is scant. To the extent that there is reason for this concern, the best solution is the elimination of legal barriers to, and constraints on, the entry of alternative suppliers of financial services—less regulation, rather than more.

To summarize, concerns for the possible negative effects of externalities support only regulation and supervision of financial institutions with government-insured deposits; of insurance companies that provide government-mandated, noncontracting third-party policies (such as for automobiles); and, possibly, of insurance companies that offer long-term life insurance and annuities.[2]

*Consumer protection.* This is the third putative justification for regulating financial services. Four aspects of consumer concern are analyzed: (1) safety-and-soundness regulations; (2) protection against fraud and misrepresentation; (3) protection against unfair treatment and insufficient information (a basic goal of the newly created UK Financial Services Authority); and (4) prevention of invidious discrimination against individuals. The first was once relevant for banks but is no longer, because deposit insurance protects people who might not be able to evaluate the solvency of these depositories. It has validity, though, for some insurance companies. The second is relevant, but it is much less of a problem for financial services than for many (perhaps most) other products that represent a greater part of the expenditures and wealth of consumers. Regulation is neither necessary nor desirable to achieve the goals of the third. Although the fourth aspect is relevant, it is neither unique to nor more prevalent in financial institutions.

*Appeal to popularly elected legislators.* This appeal to lawmakers, the fourth reason for financial-services regulation, results from their constituents' fear of financial panics and economic depressions. These are associated with bank failures and price collapses on securities markets—the costs to them when a financial-services supplier fails—and with these constituents' belief that they should pay "fair" prices and get good quality and reliable service from financial-services providers.

Each of these rationales is analyzed and found wanting. Financial panics and economic depression have indeed been associated with bank failures and stock market crashes, but are not caused by them. The failure of a financial-services firm, while somewhat costly to those directly associated with it (other than shareholders), is less disruptive than the failure of many (perhaps most) other firms of equivalent size. Similarly, intangible financial products are generally less difficult for consumers to understand and compare than are many other commonly purchased tangible nonfinancial products. Indeed, if regulation is beneficial to consumers (net of the costs of regulation, which all consumers also pay), there is more reason to regulate many other firms and products.

*Benefits to regulated financial institutions.* This is the fifth reason for regulating financial services. These institutions *might* benefit from improvements in efficiency, *do* benefit from greater consumer confidence in their products, and *greatly* benefit from protection from competition by alternative sources of financial products. The last benefit is illustrated in chapter 2 with examples from the United States, including laws and regulations that limit chartering and branching, separate commercial and investment banking, and restrict deposit-interest payments. The benefit to financial-services producers from reduced competition is one of the most important modern reasons why governments have imposed regulations on financial services.

**Intended and Unintended Costs of Regulation.** Chapter 3 analyzes the costs of regulation, both intentional and unintentional. The intended costs are those that could reasonably have been envisioned by people favoring the legislation on which the regulations are based. These include the direct expenses of the regulatory agencies and costs imposed on regulated firms, both of which ultimately are paid by consumers. Unintended costs are those that the initial supporters and drafters of the legislation probably did not foresee or were willing to discount, because the events giving rise to them were not expected to occur or were expected to be incurred at some distant time. These include:

- greater banking-system instability, because regulatory restrictions prevent banks from diversifying effectively
- escalation of regulatory costs beyond the level originally intended, because of the rewards and penalties faced by regulators
- costs to financial institutions of regulations that no longer benefit them, because of technological and market changes
- the cost to consumers and to the economy of not having the opportunity to purchase better and less costly products that would have been offered in the absence of regulation

**Optimal Regulation of Financial Services.** Chapter 4 describes how financial services could be optimally regulated. The analysis in earlier chapters reveals that the amount of regulation of financial services and financial-services firms that is beneficial to consumers should be limited to reducing negative externalities from government-provided deposit insurance, from government-mandated third-party liability insurance, and from lower-than-optimal public use of life insurance and annuities. Also, the government should protect consumers from fraud, unfair dealing, and invidious discrimination.

The experience of almost all countries in the late twentieth century shows that governments guarantee some or all of depositors' funds, whether or not they have adopted a formal deposit-insurance system. Nevertheless, the associated negative externalities can be virtually eliminated with a regulatory system that has three parts. First, there should be a substantial capital requirement that serves to absorb losses which otherwise might be imposed on depositors, and which motivates capital holders, whose investments are at risk, to monitor bank operations. This requirement can be met at low cost with respect to both capital and regulatory burden. Second, periodic reports of assets, liabilities, and capital should be presented to the authorities. Third, early intervention and resolution should be prespecified and structured.

The first requirement is met by explicitly including, under the category of "capital," uninsured debt that is subordinated to the claims of depositors and the deposit-insurance fund, and that cannot be redeemed by a bank for at least two years. This provision makes banks' capital no more costly than the capital maintained by other corporations, because it does not limit banks' access to the tax deductibility of interest expense (as would an equity requirement). The interest paid on subordinated debt and banks' problems of refinancing maturing debt also provide the authorities with market-based information on banks' financial problems.

The second requirement, several provisions of which are described in chapter 4, is also imposed to assure the authorities that the amount reported as a bank's equity capital actually reflects its economic ability to absorb losses. Financial reports, attested to at year's end by independent public accountants, permit the authorities to monitor banks' adherence to the capital requirement.

The third requirement, structured early intervention, stipulates that as a bank's capital declines below a series of prespecified percentages of its assets, the authorities first may and then must intervene to restrain expansion and the outflow of resources. Resolution—sale, merger, liquidation, or takeover of a severely capital-deficient bank—must be undertaken before the bank becomes economically insolvent. This system should result in few failures of depository institutions and, more important, little cost to the deposit-insurance fund or to taxpayers when institutions do fail.

In lieu of the capital requirement, deposits held by banks or by firms not chartered as banks could be secured with collateral. This alternative would allow nonbanks to offer fund-transfer and deposit-like savings accounts to people who might claim that they thought their funds were government-insured. As with the capital and structured early intervention and resolution (SEIR) requirement outlined for depositories, little cost would be imposed on either suppliers or taxpayers.

Insurance companies would similarly be required to hold capital sufficient to fulfill their obligations, should the value of their assets decline. Their capital would be subjected to the structured early intervention and resolution system described for banks. Insurance companies' estimates of liability to beneficiaries of third-party liability policies, life insurance, and annuities should be attested to by independent actuaries. The companies should also render periodic reports to the authorities, attested to by independent public accountants. Although accountants might occasionally conduct poor (and, very rarely, fraudulent) audits, they can be penalized, unlike government officials, by substantial economic and personal costs as a result of lawsuits and detrimental publicity. Regulators can subject these data to statistical tests, to monitor the regulated companies' financial condition.

The proposed system does not require the operationally costly and conceptually questionable administrative risk adjustments to capital requirements that have been imposed on banks and insurance companies. For example, the Basel risk-adjusted capital requirements place all loans in a single risk category, whether the loans are made to a substantial, well-capitalized company or to a risky start-up enterprise. This is done largely because a finer grouping is difficult, unstable, and, in many instances, politically unfeasible. Nor is international harmonization of regulations either desirable or necessary, despite the increasingly important internationalization of banking, securities transactions, and insurance. Cooperation among national regulators could be useful, however, if it were directed toward restraining fraud and reducing the authorities' and investors' information costs.

Consumer protection would be most efficiently conducted either generally (along with other products and services) or with special-purpose bureaus, rather than through regulation of financial institutions and markets. Indeed, combining consumer protection with regulation tends to deflect the attention of government agents away from examining, evaluating, and acting on valid consumer complaints. The combination also works to the detriment of consumers, because regulators tend to adopt the viewpoint of those they regulate and to neglect the complaints of ordinary consumers, with whom they rarely come in contact.

The proposed system could be implemented at very low cost to financial-services producers, with savings for consumers, taxpayers, and the economy in general. But protected producers and government bureaucrats would lose, and in their own self-interest they would fight vigorously to oppose the new system.

# 2

## ⌘

# *Reasons for Regulating Financial Services*

Five reasons and justifications can be delineated for subjecting financial services to governmental regulation:[3]

- benefits to government and to those in power from direct and indirect taxation of financial institutions and services
- concern about negative externalities—costs borne by people other than those who deal directly with financial institutions that fail or perform poorly
- protection of consumers from the loss of their investments, fraud and misrepresentation, unfair treatment and insufficient information, incompetent employees of financial-services providers, and invidious discrimination
- benefits to popularly elected officials from appearing to have taken measures that benefit consumers and "solve" serious problems
- benefits to the regulated financial institutions, including greater efficiency and consumer confidence (which also could benefit consumers), along with protection from competition by alternative sources of financial services (which is costly to consumers)

To evaluate proposals to eliminate, reduce, or increase regulation, it is important to understand why the institutions that produced the most important and pervasive financial product—money—were regulated by governments long before other businesses and products were regulated. Analysis of the early history of regulation shows that, in large measure, the current system of regulation was imposed to benefit monarchs and government officials at the expense of consumers.

## Benefits to Government from Regulation—Seigniorage

Perhaps the first and, in many respects, still most important financial service is the transfer of claims over resources with money. Money—an asset that is accepted by people in exchange for goods and services because they expect that others will, in turn, accept this asset for other exchanges—is an incredibly valuable financial service. It permits people to overcome the alternative of barter, which entails the substantial costs of search and information, as people try to find and evaluate goods and services that they might trade. Barter also involves the cost of storing physical goods. Money serves as an inexpensive store of value—a means by which people can efficiently delay and control their ownership and consumption of goods, and can take advantage of bargains and other opportunities. The asset used as money becomes the *numéraire*, the unit against which the prices (exchange rates) of other assets and liabilities are measured.

Over the centuries, many assets have been used as money. Commodities such as metals (principally gold, silver, and copper), leather, cows, and particular seashells, all of which had a predictably limited supply as well as an intrinsic value, were first accepted as the means of payment and store of value. Because of the cost of establishing the intrinsic value of such commodities each time they were exchanged, coins came into usage and were accepted at more than their value as a commodity. The difference between the commodity and the face value of money, called seigniorage, is a benefit that producers of money can capture. Paper money is preferable to coins because it is almost weightless. But until people had reason to believe that the currency would be accepted by others at face or at least predictable value, it was not accepted. Coins, by contrast, could be melted down and reverted to their commodity value.[4]

Governments have had a comparative advantage in producing money for two reasons. First, they can declare it to be legal tender—acceptable for the payment of taxes and fulfillment of contracts that might be enforced by their courts. Second, governments have the power to punish counterfeiters. Considering the enormous value to people of money and the gains to governments from seigniorage, one might expect that governments would produce money almost without limit.

Although the production of coins is limited by the value of the commodity used to make the coins, production can be increased by debasing new coins—mixing in a cheaper, heavy, "base" metal, such as lead. Two factors have constrained debasement. One is competition among governments when there is trade among sovereign states. When traders learn that coins are not what they purport to be, they will revalue the coins by weighing and testing them (which is costly) or by accepting only honest coins in exchange for goods. The result is the opposite of Gresham's Law—good coins tend to drive out the bad as long as people have a choice over which coins they will accept in exchange. When a government has control over most trade and can make its coins legal tender, however, it becomes a monopolist, and bad coins drive out the good (which are melted down for their commodity value or saved). The second constraint, faced by any monopolist, then comes into play. To the extent that people can substitute other products for the monopolist's product, a wealth-maximizing money monopolist would limit production of money to the amount where the diminishing marginal gains from seigniorage (as people used alternative means of making payments) equaled the cost of producing the coins.

Some history illustrates these points. Probably as a means of assuring potential users that the government would not over-expand its money supply, government-produced coins used commodities that had intrinsic value and that were in short and predictable supply—notably gold, silver, and copper. The first coins, produced in the late eighth century BCE in the Greek city-state Lydia, used electrum, a natural alloy of gold and silver. Other city-states in the Mediterranean area then produced coins. Because they competed with each other for trade, they had strong incentives to keep their coinage "honest" and not cheat by adulterating the scarce metal in their coins with base metal. When Athens obtained dominion over the area, however, its coins became the sole legal tender. It was the Athenian leader Solon (circa 630–560 BCE) who debased the coins, thereby initiating perhaps the first government-caused inflation. The inflation reduced the real debts of Solon's supporters. In a ploy repeated by politicians throughout history, Solon blamed the inflation on greedy businessmen and then punished them for having raised prices.

When nation-states evolved in which most trade was internal, governments gained monopolies over coinage. People could still, however, use the alternatives of commodities (gold, silver, copper, and leather) and paper (goldsmith receipts and bank notes). I suggest that the initial regulation of financial services was undertaken by governments to increase the revenue from seigniorage that monarchs and their officials could garner.

In sixteenth-century England, goldsmiths came to realize that the people to whom they had given receipts for gold they held for safekeeping were using the receipts as money. The receipts were accepted as money, because the holders found they could be redeemed on demand for gold. But when the receipts were used as money, only a fraction was redeemed at any one time, permitting the goldsmiths to lend out the "surplus" gold. Thus, they engaged in fractional-reserve banking, which resulted in a multiple expansion of the money (gold receipt) supply and in interest-earning loans. Unexpected demands could be met with inter-goldsmith arrangements, similar to modern correspondent banking. Furthermore, competition among goldsmiths led to their paying interest rather than charging fees for the safekeeping service. Consequently, government-produced coins, which bore no interest but did bear the risk of debasement, suffered from competition. It appears that this competition led the English government to require goldsmiths to hold 100 percent reserves or suffer execution—a rather extreme form of regulation.

Another alternative to government-produced money is notes produced by banks. Similar to the goldsmiths' gold receipts, bank notes were redeemable on demand in specie—gold and silver. Hence, the notes of banks that were trusted became the dominant form of money. Rather than attempt to beat the banks, governments, in effect, joined them: the monarch and his powerful ministers and supporters became stockholders. Governments also forced banks to share the seigniorage by requiring them to make loans to the government and its friends on favorable terms, or that might not be repaid. The amount of seigniorage that could be extracted from banks could be maximized, if the banks were given monopolies. Although it is not possible to document the causal relationship, it is probable that bank entry was restricted by governments for this reason.

In the United States, until the Banking Act of 1864 established national bank charters, only the individual states issued charters.[5] In most states, bank charters were considered to be valuable licenses, particularly after the over-issuance of paper currency by the Revolutionary War Continental Congress caused money issued by the government to be suspect. (A popular belittling phrase was "not worth a Continental.") A limited number of bank charters were issued via legislative bills, for which payments in one form or another—by political contributions or bribes, for instance—were presumably paid to legislators.

Chartering authority was restricted to the states, which did not permit banks chartered by other states to open branch offices; hence, there was a demand for banking charters. To meet public demand, legislatures in several states passed "free banking" acts. Although entry was relatively unrestricted, the banks had to back their notes with state bonds, another form of seigniorage capture. Banks chartered by the federal government ("national banks") similarly had to collateralize their notes, with U.S. government bonds. Indeed, this method of financing the Civil War is the major reason that national (federal) chartering was established. That is why the regulator of national banks, the Comptroller of the Currency, reports to the secretary of the Treasury.

Governments can still obtain seigniorage from the currency and coin they produce, but the amount is limited to the amount of currency and coin that people choose to use in place of demand deposits and other forms of transferring claims to resources. The principal benefit from inflation that can be garnered by governments, therefore, is a reduction of the real value of government bonds, assuming that the inflation was not expected when the bonds were sold, and an increase in progressively determined income taxes as a result of "bracket creep."[6]

In either event, regulation of financial institutions or financial services is essentially irrelevant for the purpose of enhancing government revenues, with three exceptions. The first is the requirement that banks hold non-interest-bearing reserves with the central bank in excess of the amount they would otherwise hold for check clearance. Earnings on these funds are usually transferred to the Treasury. This tax can be effective as long as demand deposits may be offered only by banks and there are few viable alternatives to the demand-deposit service. Until the 1980s, when savings banks and loan associations, credit unions, and brokerage firms increasingly offered checking services, this was the situation in the United States. At present, perhaps to enhance the competitiveness of demand deposits, the Federal Reserve has reduced required reserves to the amounts that banks would probably maintain voluntarily.

The second requirement is the imposition of a direct tax on bank profits. The third exception, one used by many countries, is an indirect tax in the form of forcing banks to make loans at lower than the market interest rate to government, to government-sponsored firms or projects, or to favored sectors, firms, and people. The U.S. Community Reinvestment Act, which requires banks to make loans to "deserving" people who presumably would otherwise not be adequately served, is an example. More direct wealth reallocation of this kind has been practiced extensively in Communist and former Communist countries, in various other dictatorships and "kleptocracies," and in centrally managed developing countries.

There is reason to believe that such directed lending is responsible for the failures of banks in Korea and Indonesia. These "banking crises" have been misidentified as a consequence of "lax" regulation. But the opposite is the case. Banking insolvency resulted from governmental interference or direct participation in banking decisions, rather than from poor oversight of decisions made by independent bankers who were attempting to maximize their shareholders' wealth. Decisions made by privately owned and controlled banks, however, can result in costs imposed on the economy and people of a country, which might justify government regulation. I consider these externalities next.

## Concern about Possible Negative Externalities

It is generally recognized that negative externalities, such as air pollution from gasoline-using vehicles or water pollution from farm-chemical runoffs, represent an economically valid basis for regulation. This conclusion assumes, of course, that the costs of regulation do not exceed the benefits from reducing the negative externalities, and that people cannot efficiently make transfer payments, as described by Ronald Coase (1960). Six possible negative externalities might be ascribed to the failure of financial institutions or of financial services and markets:

1. The failure of a financial institution might impose costs on noncontracting third parties.

2. The failure of a financial institution might result in runs on other solvent institutions, which would be costly to them and might cause them to fail.

3. Failures of financial-services firms might result in the collapse of the payments system, securities markets, and other important aspects of the financial system, with the result that there could be a serious adverse effect on the economy generally.

4. The failure of an institution with deposits explicitly or implicitly insured by the government, or the failure of insurance companies, might impose costs on taxpayers.

5. Concerns about the solvency of financial institutions and the terms and risks of financial instruments might impose unnecessarily high information costs on potential users and hence result in financial instruments being used less than is optimal.

6. Poor performance by financial-services providers might result in potential borrowers in the providers' market areas being badly served, with negative effects on other people and businesses in these areas.

As is shown below, only the fourth and fifth of these possible negative externalities, and an aspect of the first (noncontracting third-party insurance), provide economically valid reasons for regulating financial services.

## Imposing Costs on Noncontracting Third Parties

A noncontracting third party is someone who is negatively affected by the actions of a firm or person, but who cannot enter into a contract with that person to mitigate the harm. An example of a negative effect is the cost borne by people in a community served by only one bank if that bank fails and, as a result, recalls its demand loans to local firms which, consequently, fail and fire their employees. Another example is that of an insurance company that is unable to pay a claim made by the victim of an accident caused by a policyholder. These situations result in negative externalities, because the people who bear the costs of the bank's or insurance company's failure could not have taken actions that would have offset the costs or compensated them for the costs.

In contrast, the costs to the customers and employees of a failed financial institution should not be considered as externalities. They can take into account the possibility that the institution might fail and accordingly adjust the price they pay for loans, the interest they demand for deposits, and the wages they accept. They are contracting third parties. Similarly, although the failure of a life insurance company might inflict costs on the beneficiaries of a policyholder, the person who took out the policy can take this possibility into account when deciding which company to use. The extent to which it might be less costly for a government agency to monitor insurance companies is considered later in this chapter.

It might be argued, however, that a financial institution's customers and employees cannot adequately estimate and adjust for the risk that it might fail. Consequently, the argument goes, the government should see to it that financial institutions do not fail, or should compensate consumers and employees if they do. When the cost of the compensation is borne by taxpayers, it would represent an externality—prevention might be less costly than bailouts.

But this justification for government intervention, to the extent that it is valid, applies with much less force to financial-services firms than to many other companies, because the failure of a financial-services firm is much less disruptive to its customers or employees than is the failure of many other nonfinancial firms. For example, consider the failure of a washing machine manufacturer. Owners of its products will find obtaining repairs more costly and, after a while, not possible. Some engineers and machinists who specialize in washing machines will have to be retrained, and salespeople will lose their contacts. If this example seems trivial, given the cost of a washing machine, consider a passenger vehicle. If the manufacturer fails, not only will consumers find it difficult to obtain repairs, but the resale value of this expensive asset is likely to decline substantially. Employees of vehicle manufacturers would be substantially disadvantaged, because they often have considerable firm-specific knowledge and seniority that is not readily transferred to other firms.

In contrast, one bank is very similar to other banks, both in products and in process. A failed institution can be readily taken over by another bank, such that neither its customers nor most of its employees would be much affected. The same can be said for other financial-services firms, such as business and consumer lenders, insurance companies, and securities firms. (This issue is examined in a detailed discussion later in this chapter.) Consequently, unless one is prepared to argue that all firms should be prevented from failing, this possible externality should not be considered further.

The possible externality from the failure of the sole provider of financial services to a community or nation, should this be the situation, can be readily eliminated by removing the barriers to entry of other suppliers.[7] Indeed, with respect to banking, this has already occurred, except in some small countries that restrict the entry of foreign banks. Deposit banking in the United States and many other countries can be conducted by mail and through automatic teller machines (ATMs), the telephone, and the Internet, which permit depositors to obtain, deposit, and transfer funds from and to almost any bank from almost any location. Other financial products can be obtained from a wide range of firms, some of which are regulated and some of which are not. The European Union (EU) now permits financial-services firms to open offices and offer products in any EU country, if they are permitted to do so in their own country. Consequently, the externality that might result from the failure of a sole provider of financial services is no longer present in the EU or in the United States.

The only relevant negative externality of which I am aware,

caused by the failure of an individual financial-services firm, relates to insurance purchased in accordance with a law to protect noncontracting third parties, such as automobile-liability insurance. Those who might be injured have no way of determining whether the insurance company is solvent and will honor its contract. Consequently, if they are injured and the insurance is worthless, taxpayers, for whose protection a mandatory insurance law is designed, will probably have to pay the costs of the injury.

## Financial-Institution Failures and Runs on Other Solvent Institutions

Fractional-reserve banking is potentially fragile, because banks do not hold sufficient liquid assets with which to pay all depositors who might demand their funds. Although a solvent bank might be able to sell assets and borrow funds sufficient to meet withdrawal demands, the attempt could be so costly as to render it insolvent. An insolvent bank, by definition, cannot repay all deposits. Hence, depositors who are tardy in withdrawing their funds will suffer losses. This is the reason for runs on insolvent banks.

But why might depositors run on solvent banks? Some academic commentators point to depositors' difficulty in evaluating the economic value of bank assets, which results in their removing deposits simply on the rumor that these values have decreased below the value of a bank's liabilities: better safe than sorry. Douglas Diamond and Philip Dybvig (1983), in particular, base their argument for bank regulation on the observation that banks lend to firms and to people who cannot efficiently communicate their financial situations to the market. As Diamond (1984) puts it, banks are "delegated monitors." This makes bank loans and, hence, a large portion of bank assets "opaque."

As a result of this opaqueness, depositors are presumed to have a tendency to panic upon hearing a rumor that their bank might be insolvent. Although the assets of other firms are also opaque, creditors who fear for the solvency of firms that are indebted to them generally cannot remove their funds on demand—they cannot run. Nevertheless, creditors who fear that a firm may be insolvent because similar firms are found to be so could refuse to re-lend their funds when they mature, which could result in these firms having to sell assets or borrow at very high rates, similar to the situation faced by banks. In this regard, banks are not different from other firms with short-term liabilities.

Moreover, the financial statements of banks and other financial-services firms are much more informative than are the statements reported by many, perhaps most, other large firms. Nevertheless, investors purchase and hold the uninsured debt of these nonfinancial firms. Consider, first, banks' balance sheets. Most of their liabilities are short-term deposits and borrowings that are stated at close-to-market values. On the asset side, investments tend to be in marketable instruments that can be and, in many countries, are stated at market values. Consumer loans are almost always made up of a large number of loans for which the default risk can be determined with a high degree of accuracy. Loans to most domestic government entities are almost riskless. Fixed assets (such as buildings and equipment) make up a relatively small proportion of total assets.

This leaves commercial, agricultural, and industrial loans, which indeed are opaque. Independent chartered or certified public accountants who have access to information on individual loans, however, are charged with attesting to the reasonableness of allowances for losses on these loans. In addition, banks report the amount of their nonperforming loans, and these reports provide useful information on possible future credit losses. Although banks are faced with interest-rate risk if the durations (a present-value-weighted measure of maturity) of their assets and liabilities are unbalanced, this risk is not often a problem for commercial banks, which tend to make loans with variable (floating) interest rates.

Now compare banks' financial statements with those of non-financial companies. For example, consider the difficulty for anyone (including internal accountants and managers) to determine the market value of intangible assets—such as patents, research and development, advertising, and customer goodwill—which are not even reported as assets on financial statements unless they were purchased. Or consider the difficulty of determining the market value or the value to the firm of specialized fixed assets. Nonspecialized fixed assets and inventories might be valued at market prices, but they are included in financial statements at historical cost. These assets are often relatively large parts of nonfinancial firms' assets. Furthermore, consider the diversity and often uniqueness of the operations of many firms. In comparison, the operations and financial statements of banks, securities firms, and insurance companies are transparent.

Contrary to the claims of some academic commentators, then, the incorrectly presumed special opaqueness of banks' financial statements is not an important problem for their creditors or investors. Indeed, banks would be much less prone to failure than would many other firms, were it not for two factors. One is that, unlike the liabilities of other firms, banks' principal liabilities, deposits, can be withdrawn at par at any time; that is, they are very short-term. This may be considered a source of strength, however, particularly in the years before governments stood ready to bail out depositors. By offering depositors the right to withdraw their funds in full on demand, banks were advertising that they were being operated prudently, so that depositors would not want to take advantage of this right.[8] The principle is similar to that of firms offering consumers "double their money back" if purchasers are not satisfied with their product.

The second factor is that most banks' capital (equity plus uninsured debt that cannot be withdrawn on demand) makes up such a small proportion of their assets that a relatively small loss can result in the banks' becoming insolvent. This was not always the case. Before depositors relied on government for protection, banks maintained much more substantial capital-to-asset ratios; in fact, banks used to advertise prominently the amount of their capital and surplus. But deposit insurance (de jure or de facto) has permitted banks to hold much lower, indeed, dangerously lower, amounts of capital. I deal with this issue in chapter 4.

In fact, as George Kaufman (1994) has shown, damaging runs on banks by depositors not insured by the government have been rare. Depositors must balance the losses that might be incurred if they do not run against the costs of running, which include the loss of a valued relationship with their banker. Hence, they are unlikely to run unless they have good reason to believe that their bank is, in fact, insolvent. Indeed, Charles Calomiris and Joseph Mason (1997) found this to be the case at Chicago banks in the early 1930s, at the height of a banking panic. Although not then protected by deposit insurance, depositors did not run from solvent, though similar, banks. More recently, when Continental Illinois Bank was in danger of failing in 1984, Benston et al. (1986) found that depositors with largely uninsured deposits did not run from other large banks.

In addition, bankers sensibly make prearrangements to borrow funds should they experience unexpected withdrawals. If unprepared solvent banks that experienced runs were bailed out by a government agency, this incentive would be blunted, if not lost entirely. Nevertheless, the sooner insolvent banks are closed by depositors, the better. Such prompt closings (previously called suspensions, because banks suspended bank note redemptions) reduce the possibility that an insolvent bank might gamble for solvency by taking great risks in the hopes of recovering, even though the investments have negative expected present values. (As George Kaufman has pointed out to me, this may be why, before deposit insurance, banks could hold lower ratios of capital to assets than most other similarly sized firms.)

In any event, in countries where governments have given depositors de jure or de facto deposit insurance, runs by covered depositors have not occurred. Deposit insurance, however, has brought with it moral hazard (as insured depositors are no longer concerned about risks taken by their banks) and agency problems (as the banking authorities delay closing banks, thereby imposing costs on taxpayers). These potentially costly attributes of deposit insurance can provide a justification for regulation. The issue is discussed in this chapter, below.

Nondepository financial institutions do not operate on the basis of fractional reserves. Securities firms, for example, might hold their customers' securities for safekeeping and convenience. Should a securities firm appear to be insolvent, its customers might want to withdraw their securities. But because they have claims for specific securities, they have no reason to run, as do bank depositors; an immediate request for withdrawal would not affect the priority of their claims against the securities firm. In addition, in the United States, a government-sponsored agency provides investors with $500,000 of insurance for losses resulting from fraud or misuse of the customer securities held by the firms.

Consequently, the possibility that there would be contagious runs on solvent financial institutions (including banks and other depositories) because of the failure of one or more institutions is not supported either by logic or by experience. I conclude, therefore, that this argument for regulating financial-services firms is not valid, and turn next to what many consider to be a related and more important concern—a systemic collapse caused by the failure of financial-services firms, particularly depositories.

## Failures and the Collapse of Parts of the Financial System

In the absence of a central bank that does its job correctly, fractional-reserve banking is vulnerable to systemic collapse if there is a sufficiently large outflow of reserves (base money). Should this occur, weak banks are *likely* to fail, and even prudently run, solvent banks *could* fail. In the United States, before the creation of the Federal Reserve, several occurrences of gold outflows resulted in such collapses, as shown by Ellis Tallman and Jon Moen (1994). A central bank can offset reserve outflows with open-market operations, however, thereby preventing a multiple contraction of the money supply and a systemic financial collapse. Indeed, with the exception of the United States in the 1930s, most central banks had learned this lesson by the twentieth century, as is documented by Anna Schwartz (1986).

Furthermore, should depositors withdraw their funds from banks they believe are insolvent and not redeposit them in other banks—in other words, run to currency—the central bank can offset this decline in base money with purchases of assets from the public (open-market operations). Unfortunately, the Federal Reserve failed to take this action in the early 1930s, allowing the broad money supply (M2—demand plus time deposits) to decline by a third. The situation was made worse when people expected the incoming Roosevelt administration to demonetize gold and raise its price substantially. The consequence was a run on gold held as reserves by banks and the Federal Reserve, which further collapsed the money supply and led to the massive closing of banks in March 1933 (the "bank holiday"). These events prolonged the Great Depression, since the nation's principal means of payment and source of loans was disrupted.

The failure of depository institutions need not disrupt the payments system, however, if participants in the system are required to maintain sufficient capital to absorb possible losses and have to clear or net payments quickly or immediately (in real time). That is the way privately run payments systems operate. An example in the United States is Clearing House Interbank Payment System (CHIPS), which nets payments. Furthermore, if government regulation were not employed to constrain alternatives to bank-provided payments, the payments system would be even less vulnerable to bank failures.

Other providers of financial services do not operate with fractional reserves. Hence, the failure of one or more such firms cannot cause a systemic collapse. For example, consider the failure of a major securities firm that results in people's fearing that other, similar firms might fail. People might stop doing business with these other firms and might withdraw the securities these firms are holding for them, to place the securities with "safe" firms. Although this would be disruptive to the firms viewed as unsafe, the market for securities would not be much affected—it would lead only to a shift of business among securities firms. As is discussed below, that is likely to be less costly than the failure of many (perhaps, most) similarly important nonfinancial firms.

The October 1987 drastic fall in securities prices and the possibility of a resulting financial crisis might be seen as a situation that called for and was rectified by governmental intervention. When stock prices in the United States declined by about 30 percent in a few days, many people feared (or said they feared) that there would be a "liquidity crisis," as investors sought to sell their stocks before prices declined further. The situation was exacerbated by the breakdown for two-and-a-half hours of the Federal Reserve's system through which banks transferred reserves (Fedwire) and by overnight delays in crediting gains to "winners." The Federal Reserve is said to have prevented a liquidity crisis by exhorting banks to make loans that exceeded their normal limits and for which the value of the securities used as collateral was uncertain, thereby providing bank officers with "cover." The Federal Reserve also substantially increased general liquidity by lending to banks that made loans to securities firms which had purchased securities from panic-driven investors.

Although the costs to securities firms of the 1987 market crash might have been greater had the Federal Reserve not intervened, there is little reason to believe that the Fed actually averted a financial crisis. In particular, it is doubtful whether the Federal Reserve's publicly announced and much praised willingness to lend to banks so that they could extend loans to securities firms did much more than transfer taxpayer wealth to the banks, to the extent that the Federal Reserve's loans were at lower-than-market rates. Aside from the benefits of these loans to offset an overnight imbalance in payments, a "crisis" was not averted because there was no crisis to avert.

Consider the actions of securities firms when securities prices dropped. If firms believed that prices would decline further and could not find buyers for stock offered to them, why would they purchase the stock for their own accounts, thereby assuming losses, even if banks offered to lend them the funds? If they did so, they would absorb expected losses plus interest on the bank loans. I expect, rather, that prices fell only until enough investors thought that stocks were a bargain, at which point buy orders came in and prices stabilized. Apart from the very short-term fund-flow problem, the 1987 market crash was simply a change in expectations that hurt some people and benefited others. There were very few failures of securities firms. Certainly, there was no possibility of a systemic failure. Perhaps most important for the "consumer protection" justification, the Federal Reserve's actions were in no way "regulatory," since the Fed acted in the absence of any specific regulations and could have offered its support, whether or not banks or securities firms were regulated.

Avoiding or mitigating the possibility of systemic failure, therefore, is not a valid reason for regulating financial-services firms. Liquidity crises, to the extent that they occur, can be dealt with effectively by a central bank that has no regulatory powers or responsibilities. Only the central bank can provide liquidity to the economy when it has been substantially reduced (although, at times, central banks have oversupplied liquidity, causing an inflation, or undersupplied it, causing a depression). Regulating financial institutions, markets, and products is neither necessary nor desirable for this purpose.

## Failures and the Costs to Taxpayers and Prudently Run Banks

Almost all countries insure the deposits held by chartered financial institutions from loss, implicitly or explicitly, in whole or in part. For example, the United States de jure insures deposit accounts up to a maximum of $100,000, paid for initially from a fund administered by the Federal Deposit Insurance Corporation (FDIC), to which depository institutions contribute. (If the fund were insufficient, the insurance would be an obligation of taxpayers.) Depositors in the United Kingdom are insured by a fund administered by the Deposit Protection Board, to which depositories contribute. At present, coverage is for 90 percent of deposit accounts, up to a maximum of £20,000.

Although there is reasoning and evidence to support the belief that depositors can distinguish and have distinguished among more or less risky banks,[9] few governments can withstand political demands to protect depositors from loss. In countries without formal deposit insurance there is almost no instance in which depositors incurred losses when their banks failed, because the authorities prevailed on other banks to assume all of the liabilities of the failed institution (Benston 1995a). The only contemporary exceptions are the United Kingdom, when the Bank for Credit and Commerce International (BCCI) failed, and Argentina, which has now adopted de jure deposit insurance. In some instances, however, depositors have incurred opportunity losses when access to their funds was delayed. As a result, depositors in most countries other than the United States and the United Kingdom now have 100 percent deposit insurance. Indeed, because many countries do not have explicit deposit insurance that clearly defines what is a deposit and what is a nondeposit (presumably uncovered liability), all liabilities tend to be de facto insured.

The costs of the failures are borne first by the failed bank's shareholders and then usually by other banks through assessments to replenish a deposit-insurance fund or as a result of mergers with the failed institutions. In the United States, prior to the substantial number of failures of banks and thrift associations in the 1980s, the method most used for larger banks where some depositors were not covered by deposit insurance was "purchase and assumption." In this method an insolvent institution was merged into another, similar institution, often with the monetary assistance of the FDIC.[10]

The United Kingdom followed a similar procedure when several secondary banks failed in the 1970s. When the deposit fund is insufficient to cover the losses (as was the situation in the United States in the 1980s, when thousands of savings and loan associations failed and the Federal Savings and Loan Insurance Corporation [FSLIC] itself became insolvent), taxpayers have to pay the shortfall. Such payments are made directly from taxes, indirectly through the sale of debt, or through inflation, if the central bank makes up the shortfall by lending to failed banks with reserves or by printing money. Consequently, government-provided deposit insurance can result in a negative externality.

Government-provided deposit insurance gives rise to two related costs: moral hazard and agency. A moral-hazard cost results when depositors no longer have to be concerned about the solvency of their banks.[11] To some extent, bank managers have incentives to take greater risks, because their banks' owners get all of the positive outcomes but do not absorb all of the negative outcomes should these use up the banks' capital. Should these negative outcomes cause the banks to become insolvent, the costs will be borne by the deposit insurance fund or taxpayers. There is reason to believe, however, that this aspect of moral hazard is not very great, because the bank managers individually bear considerable personal costs if they take risks that cause or appear to cause their banks to fail.

A more important cost of moral hazard is the incentive of bank owners and their managers to operate banks with relatively low levels of capital. Unlike the usual nonbanking situation, where liabilities are not government-guaranteed, a bank's insured depositors have no reason to monitor the bank's activities or to charge an interest rate that reflects the actual risk of loss. Uninsured depositors, who are usually financially sophisticated and who maintain accounts in several banks, can quickly transfer funds from a bank that might be insolvent; hence, they have to monitor a bank only when it is weak or even close to becoming insolvent. Even then, if the bank is very large, there is reason for these depositors to expect governmental intervention to prevent such runs.[12] Consequently, banks can and do operate with much less capital than otherwise comparable firms. Therefore, regulatory intervention is justified and, indeed, necessary to ensure that depository institutions hold and maintain sufficient capital to absorb almost all expected losses.

A similar, though somewhat weaker argument applies in part to insurance companies. They should have sufficient asset reserves to pay contractual claims and sufficient equity and debt capital to absorb losses that otherwise might impair their ability to meet their contractual obligations to policyholders and to their beneficiaries. In this situation, negative externalities might come from three sources. First, legislators might bail out holders of insurance policies that had been issued by insolvent companies. This has not happened often, however. Second, people who otherwise would have been covered by disaster insurance might have to be supported with government grants. (In the United States, disaster relief is provided to uninsured property owners.) Third, people might use less than the optimal amount of insurance if they feared that insurance companies might go bankrupt. Hence, they might underprovide for their futures, which would shift some of the cost to taxpayers. This situation is considered additionally below.

Agency costs are the second important negative consequence of government-provided deposit insurance. Government officials, as agents for their principals—prudently run banks that fund deposit insurance and taxpayers on whom the burden falls should the insurance fund become insufficient—should serve the principals' interests by protecting the deposit insurance fund. But government agents have strong incentives to forbear from acting quickly to close down weak and even insolvent depositories, because they incur the political cost of dealing with the shareholders, managers, employees, and customers of these firms. Of course, the cost to individual principals (other banks and taxpayers) of monitoring and criticizing the banking authorities usually exceeds the benefits they might achieve. This conclusion follows from the often noted observation that members of large groups have incentives to "free ride" on the expected or hoped-for actions of other members that benefit the group. As a result, little or nothing is done. The problem for bankers is compounded, because they are loath to criticize the government officials who regulate them.

Thus the authorities are faced with personal costs not offset by praise and other benefits if they close weak or insolvent banks. Hence they tend to put off the day of reckoning, often in the hope that conditions will improve or even that someone else will be in charge when the possibly inevitable takeover action occurs.[13] In contrast (as Kaufman [1994] has emphasized), when depositors are not protected by insurance, deposit withdrawals (runs) automatically result in the prompt closing or suspension of depositories.

The creditors of other financial-services companies, however, are unlikely to be "favored" by a taxpayer bailout. Should securities firms and investment bankers fail, there is no reason why their customers would be protected as are depositors, except to the extent already provided by investor-protection funds. Although political pressures might result in government intervention to forestall the failure of very large or presumably "important" firms, financial-services firms would be no more likely to receive such subsidies than would companies that are not regulated.

## Less-than-Optimal Use of Financial Services

Government insurance of deposits does save some depositors the cost of assessing the risk that their banks might fail. In the United States, the cost is incurred initially by government agencies that provide supervisors and field examiners. These costs, in turn, are passed on to the banks directly, in the form of assessments and fees, and indirectly, in the form of restrictions on assets and activities presumably designed to reduce the risks that banks might take. In the short run, depending on the elasticity of demand, the banks pass these costs on to their customers. In the long run, consumers must pay the costs.

If risk-assessment and monitoring are subject to economies of scale, there is a net social benefit, at least for depositors with smaller account balances. The same benefit could be achieved and could be directed more precisely to the actual beneficiaries, however, if banks purchased privately provided insurance for depositors. The depositors might then be charged the cost of the coverage, much as people pay for other insurance coverage. Private deposit insurance would be feasible if the government provided back-up disaster insurance against large-scale bank failures. This form of reinsurance is justified and necessary, because a general banking collapse would almost always be the result of inept government-controlled monetary actions. (Such a disaster occurred in the 1930s in the United States, when the Federal Reserve permitted or caused the money supply to decline.) Alternatively and preferably, the relatively high-capital, structured early intervention and resolution (SEIR) scheme described in chapter 4, if adopted, could obviate almost all the costs of government-provided deposit insurance while fully protecting depositors.

Consumers' information costs with respect to financial instruments, such as bonds and stocks, options, mutual funds, and insurance, might be reduced if information on risks, returns, costs, and the like were provided in standard formats. Required publication of some data would probably reduce consumers' information costs, thereby increasing competition and reducing misrepresentation and fraud by some producers. For example, the U.S. Securities and Exchange Commission (SEC) and the UK Companies Acts require publication of information on financial considerations given to corporate sponsors. Another example is the required disclosure of cash surrender values by life insurance companies.

These benefits might, however, be purchased at the cost of lulling consumers into believing that they do not have to make further inquiries. For example, historical-cost financial-statement numbers often provide very poor measures of the economic condition or performance of corporations. Disclosure regulations may also be used by established firms, which usually exercise considerable influence over the details of the regulations, to support requirements in which they have already invested in order to raise their potential rivals' costs. An example is the SEC's refusal to permit foreign corporations to list their stocks on U.S. exchanges unless their financial statements employ generally accepted accounting principles (GAAP) adopted by the United States.

Although there are exceptions, requiring producers of financial products to give potential investors specific information would be more costly than beneficial to consumers, for at least two reasons. First, it is highly unlikely that a government agency would or could know what information individual investors might find necessary or even useful. This information depends on the individual investor's present and prospective wealth, taste, obligations, preferences for risk, tax situation, and so forth. Second, many important variables, such as risk, have no generally accepted metrics. Government imposition of particular measures is likely to be misleading in some situations and would constrain the development of better measures.[14]

In addition, financial-services providers have strong incentives to provide potential investors with the information they require, as do the purveyors of other goods and services. Obviously, other things being equal, investors want to purchase financial instruments that offer the greatest increase in their well-being. These benefits are reduced by the costs investors must incur to evaluate investments and assess risks. Therefore, it is in the interest of producers of the instruments to reduce these investor-borne costs by determining what information investors want and by providing them with this information, when the cost of its provision to the producer is less than the cost would have been to investors. Consequently, it is likely that the optimal amount and quality of information will be offered to investors voluntarily. This subject is discussed at length below.

The only exceptions to the conclusion that voluntary disclosure is preferable to government-mandated disclosure are fraud or misrepresentation by the producer and a possible negative externality. Fraud and misrepresentation are discussed under the heading of *consumer protection*, below. The negative externality could result from less-than-optimal disclosure of information by producers of financial products. This could occur because the producers would incur the costs of developing and providing the information but would not benefit if investors used the information only to evaluate and purchase other investments. While this eventuality might occur, producers have reason to expect that investors are more likely to purchase their products if they get and use information about these products. As almost anyone in sales and advertising knows, just getting consumers to become aware of and consider a product is more than half the battle. In addition, consumers who do not receive similar information from competitive-product producers have reason to conclude that those producers have something negative to hide. Furthermore, comparative information can be and is provided by financial-information services. Consequently, there is little reason to expect that the amount and quality of voluntarily provided information will be much less than optimal, particularly when compared with government-mandated information.

A case could be made, however, for government oversight of

companies that underwrite life insurance and annuities. Consumers might investigate these companies or rely on their reputations when they purchase these long-term insurance products. Over the often long and necessarily uncertain time until an insurance company is called on to fulfil its obligations, however, the firm's investment and managerial policies could change. The asset reserves required to meet the company's obligations might not be maintained or might be dissipated, and the company's past practice of treating beneficiaries fairly might no longer be followed. Because of this uncertainty, consumers might purchase less than the optimal amount of insurance, thereby imposing costs on themselves, their beneficiaries, and possibly the state.

The question, then, is whether the cost of governmental supervision and oversight of life- and annuity-insurance underwriters, including restraints on competition, as will be discussed later, is less than the benefit to consumers—who, ultimately, also pay the costs.

## Financial-Services Providers and
## Poorly Served Consumers

If there is little competition among financial-services providers, perhaps because there is only one or a few such vendors, some consumers might not be well served or served at all. In the language of economics, monopolists price their product where marginal cost is equated with marginal revenue, rather than with average revenue (demand). They thereby fail to serve some customers who are willing to pay more than the marginal cost of the product but not as much as the profit-maximizing price the monopolists charge. The people who cannot get loans, therefore, might not purchase or upgrade houses or establish businesses, and this inactivity could negatively affect others living and working in the area. It may also be the case that some financial-services providers misperceive the risk and other costs of dealing with minorities, females, or some other group, or of providing services to some areas. And some providers might be bigots who are willing to sacrifice profits rather than to make loans to people they dislike.

The term *redlining* has been used to describe the alleged failure of financial institutions to serve run-down, inner-city areas. To combat presumed redlining, Congress enacted laws requiring mortgage lenders to report details of loans applied for, rejected, and accepted, including the location of the mortgaged properties, the amounts of the mortgages made, and the race, sex, and income of the applicants (Home Mortgage Disclosure Act of 1975, as amended).[15] Chartered depositories must also show that they have adequately served the neighborhoods in which they have offices and have adequately served small businesses and less affluent people (Community Reinvestment Act of 1977, as amended).

To determine that the provisions of these laws are being met, government employees conduct annual, on-site "compliance examinations." Banks that want to open or close branch offices or to acquire or merge with other banks—actions for which they must obtain regulatory approval—are often challenged by community groups and by competitors (although for different reasons). To avoid delays in the required approvals, challenged banks often establish funds from which subsidized mortgages and other loans to presumably deserving and underserved people are made.

These laws and the associated regulations, required reports, and compliance examinations might be justified if there were a negative externality that could be corrected efficiently. If there were unrestrained entry, however, the presumed externality would be eliminated, as wealth-maximizing, unprejudiced bankers would enter the markets and seek out underserved consumers. The appropriate response, therefore, is less rather than more regulation.[16]

## Conclusions on Negative Externalities

The first possible externality considered—in which the failure of an insurance company that provides government-mandated, noncontracting third-party policies results in a negative externality—justifies some form of governmental intervention. The second and third possible externalities, derived from the failure of one or many financial institutions, do not give rise to actual externalities. The costs resulting from such failures can be either internalized or obviated by central-bank, open-market operations.

The only substantial negative externality that might justify regulation of financial institutions is the fourth—government-provided deposit insurance. Deposit insurance gives banks and other institutions incentives to reduce the relative levels of their capital below the amounts they would have maintained if they had to deal with depositors' concerns. Deposit insurance also creates incentives for bankers to increase risk, particularly when their banks are close to being, or are, insolvent. Consequently, the banking authorities have reason to regulate depository institutions' capital and, to some extent, their activities. But deposit insurance, which largely obviates concerns about deposit runs, also gives the authorities the incentive to forbear from taking timely action to deal effectively with weak depositories. As is discussed below, pressure from competitors also results in the authorities' restraining depositories' activities for reasons other than enhancing their soundness.

The failure of insurance companies could also impose negative externalities on taxpayers. This could occur if people who were relying on insurance had to use government-provided services when the insurance company could not meet its obligations. Fear that insurance companies might become bankrupt might keep some people from providing adequately for their futures, hence becoming dependent on and supported by the taxpayers. This is the only aspect of information costs—the fifth possible externality—that justifies governmental regulation. Incentives by financial-product providers to inform and profit from potential customers, together with unrestrained entry, should provide consumers with the optimal amount of information and service, thereby also obviating the sixth possible externality as a justification for governmental regulation.

With respect to concerns about negative externalities, then, regulation and supervision of financial institutions are justified only for those who hold government-insured deposits, for insurance companies that provide government-mandated, noncontracting third-party policies, and for companies that underwrite long-term life insurance and annuities. I turn now to the argument that regulation should be imposed to protect consumers.

## Consumer Protection

Four aspects of consumer protection can be usefully distinguished: (1) safety-and-solvency regulation designed to protect investors in financial products from loss; (2) regulation designed to protect incompetent and less able consumers from fraud and misrepresentation; (3) regulation to protect consumers from unfair treatment and from receiving insufficient information; and (4) prevention of invidious discrimination against individuals.[17]

**Safety-and-Solvency Regulations.** In part, safety-and-solvency regulations were imposed on banks to assure holders of bank notes that the notes would be honored if presented for exchange to specie. This aspect of regulation might be considered a positive externality if it had the result that people were more willing to use money (Dow 1996) and if the cost imposed by regulation were less than the benefit. Private means of ensuring the quality of bank notes were also employed, however. Before the Federal Reserve monopolized the production of bank notes in 1913, competing banks in the United States presented bundles of notes late on Friday afternoons in the hope of embarrassing their rivals. To defeat this tactic and to meet ordinary customer demands, banks kept adequate reserves or made arrangements with other banks to obtain reserves at short notice. Publications (bank-note locators) were established that informed people about the notes of insolvent banks. It is not clear whether the private or the governmental means of assuring consumers was the more effective.[18]

Safety-and-solvency supervision and examination of banks could be seen as protecting depositors when checks—demand deposits or current accounts—displaced bank notes as the principal form of money. As was discussed earlier, however, the threat of runs appears to have been a stronger goad to banks' maintaining adequate reserves and capital. Indeed, the excellent record of the essentially unregulated Scottish banks in meeting the withdrawal demands of their depositors provides evidence that in a competitive situation, regulation is not necessary for consumer protection. Not only did Scottish banks rarely impose losses on depositors, but they paid interest to note holders during the period when it was necessary for them to suspend convertibility.[19]

Government-provided deposit insurance now makes this aspect of consumer protection moot, as it protects most consumers from loss. Those who are unprotected—for example, those with deposit accounts of more than $100,000 in the United States—should be able to protect themselves, much as do wealthy investors generally.

Safety-and-solvency regulations have also been imposed on insurance companies to protect purchasers and beneficiaries of long-term insurance and annuities and third-party, noncontracting beneficiaries of government-mandated insurance policies. The manner in which such justifiable regulations could be implemented efficiently is explained in chapter 4.

**Protection against Fraud and Misrepresentation.** Governments are usually expected to protect their citizens against fraud and misrepresentation. This protection might be justified on the grounds that some citizens are incapable of protecting themselves; on the belief that the government can achieve economies of scale in these actions; and because enforcement of criminal laws is a governmental monopoly. With respect to financial products, prevention of fraud and misrepresentation generally takes the form of regulations that specify what information about the terms of contracts must be disclosed and, often, how it must be disclosed to consumers; waiting periods during which contracts can be voided; and public disclosure of periodic financial data by depositories and insurance companies. At times, government agencies have been given the power to determine which financial instruments can and cannot be offered to the public. In the United States, these state-enacted Blue Sky laws generally apply to equity securities.[20]

It seems clear that government officials rarely possess all the knowledge necessary to promulgate rules that are beneficial to consumers and that govern which financial products they may or may not purchase. Mandatory disclosure is preferable to this regime. As was noted earlier, however, government officials not only cannot specify universally useful disclosure rules but also may design rules that keep financial-product producers from communicating effectively with consumers. For example, until recently, the U.S. Securities and Exchange Commission prevented publicly traded corporations from reporting the market value of traded assets, while requiring them to present essentially meaningless (from the viewpoint of economic values) historical cost data. In large measure, the SEC took this action because it was administratively easier for it to evaluate historical cost data.

Furthermore, the cost of mandatory disclosure in the United States has been very high. Direct costs include preparing and presenting a large body of data, much of which is not considered or even read by potential investors. A possibly material mistake or misstatement can result in very costly lawsuits; hence, corporations must incur substantial accounting, audit, printing, and legal fees. Indirect costs include corporations' inability to communicate effectively with shareholders and potential investors. Having reviewed a large body of empirical studies on this question, I conclude that the U.S. system of mandatory financial disclosure has, on balance, hurt rather than benefited investors.[21]

Whether or not government can reduce fraud and manipulation by regulating any business or product, there seems no reason to single out financial institutions and products. Indeed, such products are relatively easy for people to evaluate. Furthermore, most financial institutions have considerable investments in their charters and in customer goodwill. Hence, they have strong incentives to treat customers fairly. In the event that they do not, either because of corporate policy or inability to control salespersons' misstatements, they can be sued and subjected to judgments—serious inducements to reinforce corporate incentives to avoid engaging in fraud and misrepresentation. Probably of greater importance, however, is that at low cost consumers can shift their businesses from suppliers with doubtful reputations to their competitors, because similar financial products are delivered by many firms. Thus, financial-product institutions have strong incentives to maintain reputations for honesty and fairness.

That is not to say that financial products might not be misrepresented to consumers. Recently in the United States, for example, a savings and loan association (Lincoln) was charged with misrepresenting small-denomination uninsured subordinated debentures as FSLIC-insured certificates of deposit. In the United Kingdom, some insurance companies have been charged with misrepresenting or misinforming people about the net returns that might be earned on pension funds.

Whatever the merit of these claims, they should be contrasted with the potential difficulties faced by consumers in purchasing many other nonfinancial products, such as appliances, clothing, equipment, houses, and automobiles. Consumers often claim that the attributes and merits of these products were misrepresented to them or that the products did not perform as expected. In contrast with the relatively simple financial-services products, complaints about many other products cannot be successfully specified and demonstrated. Furthermore, the manufacturers of many other products often cannot be located or, if they can, do not have reputations they care to maintain. Hence, unless one asserts that *all* consumer products and their producers should be regulated, consumer protection against possible misrepresentation is not a sufficient reason to regulate financial-services providers or products.

**Protection of Consumers from Receiving Unfair Treatment and Insufficient Information.** Consumer protection is a basic goal of the UK Financial Services Authority (FSA), established in 1998, which combines the financial-services regulatory functions of nine agencies.[22] As expressed in the Report to the Chancellor (1997), which outlines the mission and structure of the FSA, the FSA's three "high-level aims" are "to protect consumers of financial services," "to promote clean and orderly markets," and "to maintain confidence in the financial system."[23] In general, the report assumes that consumer protection will be accomplished by regulating the business practices of financial-services firms.

Specifically, to achieve its first-stated, high-level aim the FSA will

> set, promote, monitor and enforce high standards of integrity, financial soundness, fair dealing and competence for those it regulates, in order to protect and secure fair treatment for investors, depositors, and policyholders.

The document continues: "[The FSA should] aim to ensure that consumers receive clear and adequate information about services products and risks," but it should "acknowledge consumers' responsibility for their own decisions." The second high-level aim asserts that

> in the first instance . . . [the FSA should look] to the market and market participants to set and enforce high standards in this area [and] should take action where such standards are inadequate or are ineffectively enforced.

To maintain confidence in the financial system, the third high-level aim, the FCA will

> set, promote, monitor and enforce high standards of financial soundness and probity for financial services businesses . . . to promote consumers' and financial institutions' confidence in its strength and integrity [and ensure] . . . that the failure of individual financial institutions does not undermine the overall stability and soundness of the financial system.

The third high-level aim can be achieved without regulation of financial-services firms by the Bank of England's use of open-market operations to stabilize the money supply. Furthermore, as discussed below, government regulation of financial services to enhance consumer confidence is either unnecessary (given deposit insurance), has little effect on consumers' willingness to participate in financial (particularly securities) markets, or is more likely to be harmful than helpful to consumers.

With respect to consumer protection, contrary to the expressed objective of the creators of the FSA, on balance it is likely to work against the interests of consumers. The validity of this conclusion may be seen from the following close examination of explicit arguments for the regulatory system envisioned by the FSA, as expressed by an eminent scholar, Professor David Llewellyn.[24] He is a coauthor of a comprehensive examination of regulatory issues (Goodhart et al. 1998) and has been a public-interest director of the UK Personal Investment Authority (PIA), "the leading regulator . . . within the Financial Services Act for retail investment services business" (Llewellyn 1995, 12). In an article describing and justifying the work of the PIA, Llewellyn (1995, 13) presents a complete and specific description of consumer-borne costs that regulation is designed to reduce or obviate.

Before subjecting his arguments to analysis, I want to express my agreement with his distinction between wholesale and retail purchasers of financial services. Llewellyn (1995, 14) presents four convincing reasons for concluding that "the case for regulation and supervision of retail financial services is more firmly based than for wholesale markets." This conclusion is echoed in Charles Goodhart et al. (1998, chapter 9, paragraph 17): "When professionals are dealing with each other the need for conduct of business regulation is less evident, and greater reliance can be placed on self-created Codes of Conduct." Just why such a "gentlemen's code" is required for financial services but not for other business dealings is not explained, although the authors are aware that such codes have at times been used to create cartels and to restrain competition. Nor do Goodhart et al. explain why, beyond laws that seek to restrain and punish fraud, breaches of trust, and violations of contracts, it is in the public interest for the government to be involved at all in relationships among firms and professionals, particularly with respect to financial services and products. Llewellyn, though, is concerned only for retail purchasers.

Llewellyn (1995, 13) justifies regulation of financial services as follows:

> The ultimate rationale of regulation designed to protect the consumer is . . . based on three principal strands of analysis:
>
> • The correctness of identified market imperfections and failures that reduce consumer welfare and distort competitive and market mechanisms.
> • Consumers can benefit from the economies of scale derived from collective authorization (via a "fit and proper" criterion) and monitoring of firms by a specialist regulator.
> • Confidence in the market can be enhanced by signaling minimum standards of quality.

With respect to the first "strand," Llewellyn presents the following extensive list of "imperfections" in the market for retail financial services that regulation would presumably correct:

problems of inadequate consumer information; problems of asymmetric information; the difficulty of ascertaining the quality of financial contracts at the point of purchase; imprecise definitions of products and contracts; under-investment in information by consumers (the "free-rider" argument where all consumers assume that others have investigated the safety and integrity of suppliers of financial services); agency costs and potential principal-agent problems and issues related to conflict of interest and, because of the technicalities of some financial products, consumers are not equally equipped with an ability to assess quality, etc.

Llewellyn's reasonably complete and well-drawn list of potential difficulties could be applied to a wide range of nonfinancial products and services. For example, purchasers of television sets, automobiles, refrigerators, computers, and other appliances have "inadequate" information about how the sets were manufactured, the time when specific parts might fail, the cost of repairing the unit, and so forth. They suffer from "asymmetric information"—they know less than the manufacturers. Consumers probably find it difficult to ascertain the quality of an offered warranty or repair contract at the time of purchase. They would probably "free ride" on other consumers' investigations and, hence, underinvest in information. Potential conflicts of interest pervade almost all retail purchases—as well as other exchanges. For example, should a store selling television sets be required to tell potential customers its profit margins, promotional incentives offered by the manufacturer, and the commission that might be paid to the salesperson? Might not a paint store recommend a poorer product on which it has a higher margin? It might be years before the consumer will find that the recommended product was incorrectly described. Nor are all consumers equally equipped to evaluate all products.

Thus, the potential market failures listed by Llewellyn apply with equal or greater force to many products and services that are not regulated. I expect (or at least hope) that neither Llewellyn nor almost anyone else would want the government to establish a Consumer Appliance Authority or Home Maintenance and Repair Authority to deal with the economic problems faced by consumers of these nonfinancial products. Rather, it would or should look to competition among suppliers and other market forces to solve the problems. Furthermore, as was discussed earlier in this chapter, financial products are generally easier for nonexpert consumers to evaluate. In addition, these products are almost always offered by institutions that have incentives to invest in and maintain reputations for fairness and honesty, and that are likely to be in business for many years.

Having provided a list of possible problems, Llewellyn continues as follows (ibid.):

> In a regulation-free environment these imperfections impose clear costs on the consumer. An informed judgment about the purchase of financial products and services cannot be made unless consumers know the true costs of the product; the precise nature and full terms of the product or contract; the basis upon which a financial product is offered (for example, whether the firm is a tied agent or independent advisor), or what the benefit is to an agent (for example, commissions.) These are real information costs to the consumer.

But, of course, the listed "imperfections" do not impose real costs on consumers, because the situations described are best dealt with by ordinary market forces. At the least, they are of greater importance for many, if not most, nonfinancial products for which regulation has not been implemented or proposed.

Llewellyn concludes (ibid.):

> A high degree of information disclosure is required in order to make consumers effective in the marketplace. If regulation requires the firm or agent to provide the necessary information then, although the costs of suppliers/agents will rise and be reflected in prices, this is not a net cost to the consumer as the objective is to offset the information costs in the previous régime.

A high degree of information is indeed required. Consumers who want to evaluate the net benefits from purchasing any product—be it a financial investment, a car, or a good meal—might implicitly or explicitly estimate the discounted net cash flows they expect to obtain from the product. Such a calculation, if it were undertaken, would require information about alternatives, translation of noncash benefits into cash equivalents, consideration of tax effects (if any), estimation of the appropriate discount rate, and so forth. In addition, the consumer would need to include the cost of obtaining the information and of making the calculations.[25] With these costs included, some (perhaps most) consumers who are making "informed judgments"—acting in their own self-interest—would find that the cost of the analysis exceeds the benefits thereof, and they would be better off relying on the reputation of the vendor or on the experiences of other consumers. Furthermore, as noted earlier in this chapter, vendors have strong incentives to inform consumers effectively about the qualities of their products and of alternatives supplied by other vendors.

Neither Llewellyn nor anyone else to my knowledge has explained why a government agency is more likely than are suppliers to determine what information consumers would find useful for making "informed" decisions. Indeed, Llewellyn points out some important costs to consumers of government regulation. First, "any costs of regulation are reflected in the price of services paid by consumers" (Llewellyn 1995, 15). Second, Goodhart et al. (including Llewellyn) point out that, because "regulation is largely perceived [by consumers] as being a free good . . . combined with risk-averse regulators, there is an evident danger that regulation is over-demanded by consumers . . . and over-supplied by the regulator" (1998, chapter 9, paragraphs 5 and 6). Third, as Llewellyn warns, consumer regulation "creates the impression that the consumer need not take care with respect to the firms with which he or she deals in financial services. This becomes a moral hazard of regulation: a hazard that regulation itself creates the image that less care need be taken" (Llewellyn 1995, 17).

An additional cost to consumers flows from Llewellyn's third "strand," on which he says regulation is also based—"confidence in the market can be enhanced by signaling minimum standards of quality." Llewellyn argues that this is a benefit, because minimum standards would keep risk-averse consumers, who cannot distinguish good from bad products at the point of purchase (because of asymmetric information), from exiting the market for financial services (Llewellyn 1995, 14). This circumstance solves the "lemons" problem, whereby people will not purchase goods that they fear may be defective. Llewellyn does not say why consumers are not driven from other markets characterized by asymmetric information—which is to say, almost all retail and many wholesale markets. Nor does he say why producers of "good" financial services would not have sufficient incentives to inform consumers about the qualities of their products and help them avoid their competitors' "bad" products.

Llewellyn does say, however, that "suppliers may also have an interest in regulation which sets minimum standards and enhances confidence in the markets" (Llewellyn 1995). It is with this "interest" that the cost to consumers enters. These suppliers also have an interest in denying consumers the opportunity of purchasing competitive, newly developed, alternative goods. High-quality suppliers similarly would benefit from consumers' not being allowed to substitute lower-quality (but less costly) goods for their products. At least since 1776, when Adam Smith published *The Wealth of Nations*, it has been recognized that minimum-standard regulations have been used for these purposes, to the detriment of consumers.

Thus, I conclude that the first and third justifications ("strands") offered by Llewellyn for regulating financial services in the interests of consumers—to correct market imperfections and to establish minimum-quality standards—are not persuasive, when all aspects are considered. This leaves the second strand—"economies of scale derived from collective authorization [via a 'fit and proper' criterion] and monitoring of firms by a specialist regulator." Llewellyn points to savings from avoiding "excessive duplication and hence excessive social costs" and "economies of scale that are derived through a specialist regulator-supervisor acquiring expertise and establishing effective authorisation and monitoring systems" (Llewellyn 1995). True, the public could benefit from a single monitor of the financial condition and practices of financial-services providers who could save them from having to incur these costs individually. Purchasers of other products, such as automobiles, machinery, appliances, and computers, could similarly benefit from having the sellers of these products monitored and supervised by a single agency. There is no reason to believe, however, that these benefits should be provided by a government agency. If there is a demand, private information publications, such as *Consumer Reports* in the United States and *Which?* in the United Kingdom for products, and *Standard and Poor's, Moody's,* and *Best's Insurance* for financial-services firms and products, can and do provide these services.

Nor, except as was concluded earlier in this chapter for depositories and for some insurance products with respect to externalities, is there reason to believe that the solvency of financial-services firms should be of special government concern. First, there is no public interest in the governmental monitoring of firms that provide investment banking, securities, loans, and other financial services, because the failure of these firms would not result in negative externalities. Second, consumers of these products have no more reason for concern about the producers' solvency than they have for the solvency of firms that produce nonfinancial products or for the continued operations of firms or people with whom consumers have continuing relationships, such as doctors, dentists, and automobile mechanics. Indeed, as was discussed earlier, the failure of many nonfinancial firms could impose greater costs on consumers.

**Prevention of Invidious Discrimination against Individuals.** In many countries it is appropriately illegal to discriminate invidiously against persons because of their race, sex, national origin, or any other personal attribute that is irrelevant to the economic decision under consideration. From an economic point of view, laws against invidious discrimination (bigotry) in the provision of publicly available services are justified on several grounds. One is that bigotry imposes information and search costs on people who are discriminated against, as they seek to learn whether, where, and how they will be served. Another is avoidance of an externality resulting from some people's belief that they are being treating unfairly—that is, for reasons unrelated to their ability to pay or produce. Antibigotry laws can also be justified on moral or ethical grounds, based on a society's concept of fairness. But the usefulness or validity of such laws is not the issue here. The issue is whether there is anything special about financial services compared with nonfinancial services that would support a greater or lesser degree of regulation with regard to invidious discrimination. From the following brief analysis, I conclude that a lesser degree of regulation is justified.

Financial institutions, particularly banks, are vulnerable to public disapproval. This probably explains why some banks discriminated against females, blacks, and other minorities when such practices were acceptable. Had they not discriminated, they would have had reason to believe that some economically more important and presumably bigoted customers would have complained and taken their business elsewhere. It is also likely that some bankers, similar to other people, were bigots who chose to discriminate.

Another possibility is that banks (and other enterprises) employed what has been termed *efficient statistical discrimination*. For example, although only some people of a particular identifiable group may be irresponsible debtors, it might be less costly for a lender to deny loans to all members of that group than to ignore this relationship. In this situation, the lender saves the costs of monitoring, collecting, and writing off bad loans which, the lender believes, are greater than the net profits that would have been made on "good" members of the discriminated-against group. Even though this analysis could be correct, in the United States the legislature has determined that it is illegal, in large measure because the economic and psychological costs to discriminated-against people and society in general are perceived as greater than the costs that might be imposed on lenders. (I agree.)

Statistical discrimination has been forcefully alleged with respect to mortgage lending in the United States. Originally (in the 1970s and 1980s) this allegation was cast in terms of geography, wherein banks (including savings banks and savings and loan associations) were said to "redline" older, run-down, often center-city areas in which poorer people and minorities tended to live. In effect, banks were supposed to have drawn a red line around these areas and to have made fewer loans than were demanded, or to have imposed onerous terms on the loans that were made.

I addressed these allegations in earlier, coauthored studies by examining data from central cities that were alleged to have been redlined and from reasonably similar suburbs, used as controls, of four U.S. cities. My coauthors and I examined loan terms and measured demand for loans with interviews of potential home sellers and home buyers, as these people would know about demands for mortgages that might not have been met (Benston, Horsky, and Weingartner 1978; Benston and Horsky 1991). We found no evidence to support the allegation of redlining. Rather, we found that home buyers got the mortgages they wanted at terms that did not differ significantly between central-city and suburban areas. Home sellers in the central cities did not experience difficulties in selling their properties because of potential buyers' inability to obtain financing. Rather, we found that banks evaluated mortgage applications individually.

Furthermore, a review of other evidence on the general question of discrimination reveals that few, if any, banks or other mortgage lenders now practice racial or geographic discrimination, directly or indirectly (Benston 1997b). In addition, financial products are, by their nature, impersonal. Consequently, there is not much opportunity for bigots who provide financial services to discriminate against people they dislike, nor are bigots likely to get much pleasure from such actions. Furthermore, competition among wealth-seeking financial institutions will probably result in these people (among others) being well served; this is the best and most reliable form of consumer protection against invidious discrimination.

**Conclusions about Consumer Protection.** An early reason for regulating and supervising financial institutions—concerns about the solvency of issuers of bank notes and holders of deposits—is no longer relevant. Bank notes are now produced by central banks, and all but very large deposits are protected by government-provided deposit insurance. The solvency of some insurance companies, though, is a valid reason for regulation.

Protection of consumers against fraud and misrepresentation and against invidious discrimination are valid governmental goals. The only thing special about financial institutions and financial instruments, however, is that they are less subject to these problems than are many other kinds of firms and products. Hence, the goal of protecting consumers does not provide a rationale for specially regulating financial services. Nor is it valid or useful to use regulation of financial-services firms and markets to protect consumers from receiving unfair treatment and insufficient information. The concerns for consumers with respect to these "problems" can be lodged even more forcefully against many (perhaps most) suppliers of consumer products. Nor is there any special reason for government to protect wholesale purchasers of financial products.

Government agencies, however, might act as ombudsmen for consumers who believed that they were misled or cheated by a financial-services provider. That is probably more cost-effective for both consumers and producers than the alternative of consumers' believing they have been mistreated or having to sue providers to get justice. Efficient implementation of this form of regulation is described in chapter 4.

## Interests of Popularly Elected Officials to "Solve" Apparent Problems

Regulations that appear to save citizens from the negative consequences of important events they do not comprehend and appear to protect them from presumably overpriced or poor-quality products and services are understandably popular with voters and, hence, with politicians. Three such situations have motivated governments to enact legislation regulating financial-services providers. The first and foremost is financial panics and economic depressions, with which bank failures have been associated. It is easy for politicians to argue that these costly events should not be permitted to occur. Second, politicians might also insist that the failure of a supplier on whom consumers, employees, businesses, and communities rely should be avoided and possibly prevented. Third, consumers should pay "fair" prices and get good quality and reliable service, particularly for products with properties that are difficult for ordinary people to evaluate. Politicians who adopt laws and regulations that appear to achieve these goals are likely to be rewarded by voters.

The brief analysis below of each of these three reasons for regulation reveals that financial-services firms and financial services are among those posing the fewest problems. Nevertheless, with the exception of health- and physical safety–related goods and services, financial-services firms and products have been more heavily regulated. Some possible reasons for this situation are given at the end of this chapter.

**Financial Panics and Economic Depressions.** Bank failures have caused financial panics and economic depressions at times when a central bank did not offset declines in reserve (base) money that resulted from exports of specie or runs to currency.[26] This problem beset U.S. banks before the Federal Reserve was established in 1913. Unfortunately, the Federal Reserve did not offset the run to currency during the Great Depression; indeed, in 1937 and 1938 the Fed increased reserve requirements, thereby exacerbating and prolonging the depression. By the end of the nineteenth century, however, European central banks had learned how to deal with money, as documented by Schwartz (1986). Indeed, the last large UK bank to have failed was the City of Glasgow Bank in 1878, which concentrated its loans on a few (director-related) borrowers. Although some large U.S. banks have failed in recent times, such as the Continental Illinois Bank in 1984, these banks could have survived had they had a little more capital to absorb their losses.

Rather than bank failures causing financial panics and economic depressions, banks commonly become insolvent when the firms to which they lend become insolvent as a result of exogenous (to banks) economic downturns. In past times and even today, banks and savings and loan associations that were directed or encouraged by government officials to lend to favored people, companies, and industries have become insolvent. (This occurs in less developed countries in Latin America, Asia, and Eastern Europe and even in some developed countries in the European Union and in the United States.)

In these situations, it was governmental regulation of banks and governmental mismanagement of the economy that caused banks to fail. Nevertheless, it is difficult for the public (including journalists) to understand the causal relationships. Hence, apparently imprudent actions taken by banks tend to be blamed for financial panics and economic disasters, and politicians benefit from enacting legislation that appears to control and punish banks. In particular, this is the origin of the laws and regulations enacted in the United States during the 1930s' Great Depression.[27]

Similarly, "lax" regulation of new securities issues and stock exchanges was blamed incorrectly for the October 1929 U.S. stock market crash, which in turn was blamed incorrectly for the 1930s' Great Depression. In fact, the decline in industrial production and wholesale prices preceded the crash, and the decline in stocks reflected rather than caused the depression. But the public hearings conducted by Ferdinand Pecora in 1933 and 1934 for the Senate Banking Committee produced a barrage of publicity blaming the depression on the questionable activities of banks and securities firms in securities underwriting and trading. Financial statements were said to have been incomplete and possibly fraudulent. I examined these allegations (particularly those related to the securities activities of banks and financial-statement disclosure by exchange-listed corporations) and found no support for the allegations (Benston 1969, 1973a, 1976, and 1990). As a result of the hearings and campaign promises by presidential candidate Franklin Roosevelt, the Congress passed the Banking Act of 1933 (the Glass-Steagall Act), the Securities Act of 1933, and the Securities and Exchange Act of 1934. This legislation was supposed to "solve" the problems. But in fact these acts made things worse for consumers and the economy.

**Failure of a Financial-Services Supplier on Which Consumers and Others Rely.** The failure of a supplier of financial services is, indeed, often costly to its customers. As was noted earlier, however, its demise is generally less costly than the failure of other companies. Unlike many other products, financial services produced by different firms are similar and can be replaced at relatively low cost. These products—demand and time deposits, consumer and commercial loans, securities underwriting and brokerage, futures and options, insurance brokerage and sales, and the like—are produced by many firms locally, nationally, and worldwide. For that reason, a failed or failing financial-services firm is often absorbed into another firm, and its customers hardly notice the change. Even if another firm did not take over an insolvent financial-services firm, if entry into financial markets were unconstrained, there is little reason to believe that the customers and employees of the insolvent institution would not be able to find close alternatives rather quickly and at low cost.

Contrast this with the consequences of the failure of a manufacturer of machinery, computers, home appliances, vehicles, or almost any other good that is not quickly consumed. How would purchasers of the assets get them serviced? Would employees whose knowledge is tied to the particular product be able to get other jobs at equivalent wages? If financial-services firms should be regulated to prevent or reduce their failure, this argument applies with much greater force to a much wider range of firms. Yet, quite reasonably, there has been no call for this sort of government regulation.

A related argument is that people who place their savings in banks or who invest in securities should not have to fear losing a substantial portion of their wealth. If this argument were valid, it should hold even more strongly with respect to assets that represent greater proportions of most people's wealth—automobiles and houses. When people get their cars repaired, they place not only their property but, to some extent, their lives at the mercy of mechanics who are unregulated. House renovations and repairs might be poorly done or not done at all, even though they were paid for. Although some consumers might learn from subsequent experience and from the experience of others something about the quality of repairs, few are expert enough to determine whether a bad outcome is the result of a bad repair, another event, or their own misuse or neglect of the car or house. Yet auto repair shops, roofers, house renovators, and the like are not regulated as are financial institutions. In these situations, which are much more important for most (particularly less affluent) people, competition among suppliers and privately generated sources of information appears to work satisfactorily. Otherwise, it is likely that legislators and bureaucrats would have enacted laws and regulations to "correct" the situation. An unregulated market would work at least as well for financial services.

**"Fair" Treatment of Consumers.** As discussed earlier, when national currency was produced by banks, their supervision and examination could be justified on the assumption that bank-note holders could not assess the risk that the notes would not be redeemed. This justification does not apply to the money now produced by banks—demand deposits (current accounts). Unlike bank notes, checks are not used as hand-to-hand currency, primarily because of the much greater risk that the depositor, rather than the bank, might be insolvent. Hence, this justification for regulating banks is no longer valid. In addition, deposit insurance now protects less knowledgeable people.

Another argument for regulation is that banks, securities

firms, insurance companies, and other financial-services firms have information about their financial services and products that is not possessed by consumers. If this were valid, there is an even more compelling reason to regulate a very large number of other products and services. As was discussed earlier, television sets, washing machines, refrigerators, air conditioners, and furnaces are much more important to most people than are financial products. The repair of these appliances, with respect to both effectiveness and price, is similarly more important than are the qualities or price of financial services. Furthermore, the features, reliability, and other attributes of appliances are more opaque than are the attributes of most financial products. In addition, the similarity of financial services provided by different firms makes it relatively easy for consumers to compare and choose among them. In comparison, most people have small deposit balances, have more wealth invested in homes than in stocks and bonds, and rely on social security for retirement rather than on savings and annuities.

Regulation of the prices of financial services has been justified on the related grounds that consumers are not able to compare prices of similar products offered by different suppliers or are unable to determine whether or not the price (or other terms) is "fair." At times, ceilings on loan-interest rates and on the rates charged for insurance have been based on this assumption. Indeed, people are often in favor of price controls, at least initially, because they believe they will benefit from purchasing goods at lower prices (for example, usury ceilings on interest rates and price controls on gasoline) or from being able to avoid having to pay higher prices (for example, rent controls). After a time, however, they generally come to realize that the quality of the price-controlled goods deteriorates, or that they are in short supply, available only to some favored people. Consequently, from the general absence of price controls, it appears that most people and, hence, most politicians come to realize that price controls are rarely beneficial to consumers.[28]

Experience (if not academic economists) teaches them that price ceilings set below market rates represent the price at which one cannot get loans or insurance. Furthermore, these ceilings impart a bias that works against poorer and riskier people, who are screened out by lenders and insurers because they are not legally permitted to offer these consumers a product priced to compensate for expected losses. The fact is that consumers are likely to get "fair" prices only when many producers vie for their trade.

The difficulty consumers might have in evaluating financial products should also be contrasted with their difficulty in evaluating other products. Such commonly purchased consumer products as television sets, houses, cars, refrigerators, and computers are much more complex and varied than are most financial products. Why, then, are financial services more extensively regulated?

People might want surety that the assets, products, and services they purchase will maintain their values and perform as expected. Nevertheless, considering that those nonfinancial products that do not directly affect people's health or safety are not regulated, it appears that people realize that the assurance they would like to have about these products can rarely be provided by government agents. This understanding may exist because it would be difficult for government employees to evaluate products that have multiple attributes and configurations designed to appeal to different tastes among consumers, and that change over time in quality and other dimensions. Furthermore, these goods are sold by many retail establishments that often offer different combinations of price and service. In contrast, financial services and products are uniform and, with the exception of life insurance and annuities, rather simple. Hence, it might seem easy for government officials to enact rules regulating financial products for the benefit of consumers.

For example, usury laws have been maintained by the states on the assumption that ceilings on interest rates would keep lenders from "gouging" borrowers. (Biblical injunctions against usury are rarely invoked as a justification for their continuance.) This constraint was overridden by a federal statute for mortgages only when, with the increase in market interest rates in the early 1980s above the usury ceilings, many ordinary people found that they could not get mortgage loans at all. Although the states may, in turn, override the federal law, none has done so, probably because consumers learned that the state law actually does not benefit them. If nominal interest rates go up sharply again, however, potential borrowers might once more clamor for a ceiling. This is a call that politicians might heed, even though the restriction would be damaging to many borrowers, particularly those who pose a greater risk to lenders. These borrowers would be the ones unable to borrow legally.

Required disclosure of the terms of financial products and of financial data about publicly traded corporations has had much appeal, since it is difficult for anyone to object to corporations having to inform consumers. Indeed, such rules are preferable to laws that specify what consumers can and cannot purchase.[29] Consumers might also believe the disclosures are costless to them. They probably do not realize that they pay the costs incurred by producers to provide the information; nor do they realize that producers are not permitted to provide them with some information they might find valuable. Hence, there is little opposition to mandatory disclosure.

Perhaps most important, although financial institutions were regulated long before consumer protection became a legislative concern, once regulated they become an easy target for those who value regulation. Legislators have often passed laws and government agencies have often developed regulations that serve to restrain competition for the benefit of financial institutions. Now other legislators and some consumer advocates argue that, having "been given" governmental benefits, financial institutions in particular should be required to be "socially responsible."

In addition, as is discussed below, some regulated financial institutions continue to benefit from regulation. Because they tend to be more highly organized and focused than do their potential competitors (who might not even come into existence because of restrictive regulations), these institutions have generally been able to influence legislators more effectively than could consumers and producers who would benefit from eliminating regulations.

## Benefits to the Regulated Financial Institutions

Financial institutions benefit from regulation in three principal respects: (1) greater efficiency from government-imposed standardization; (2) enhanced consumer confidence in the safety of their investments and in the quality of financial products; and (3) protection from competition by alternative sources of financial services. The first two may also benefit consumers; the third harms them.

**Greater Efficiency from Government-Imposed Standardization.** By imposing standardized presentation of information, government regulations might reduce data-presentation costs to financial-services firms and reduce consumers' costs of analyzing and comparing financial products.[30] Although standardization could be adopted voluntarily by firms, the firms might not be able to overcome the difficulties of achieving agreement and, consequently, would not obtain the joint benefit from complete participation—the whole is greater than the sum of the parts. An early example is standardized public reporting of the financial condition and (later) income and expense of banks and insurance companies. Financial reports required of publicly traded corporations by the Securities and Exchange Commission in the United States, and of all companies by the Companies Act in the United Kingdom, are a more general example that is supposed to benefit investors and creditors.[31]

Standard rules for valuing mutual funds, money market mutual funds (MMMFs), and cash management accounts have probably been useful in reducing consumers' information costs. For example, requiring MMMFs to state their redemption values in full dollar amounts simplifies redemptions and check writing. Rules requiring the quality and maximum maturities of short-term instruments in which MMMFs may be invested also reduce consumers' information costs and make comparisons among funds easier. Standardized reporting of operating costs that are charged to consumers, such as management fees charged by mutual-fund managers and investment costs incurred by the funds, can be useful to consumers and to more efficient firms and potential new entrants.

Standardized micro-encoding of checks would be an example of standardization that reduces producers' costs, except that this innovation was adopted by privately owned banks working through their trade associations or in concert. Casualty insurance companies in the United States have had to use the standardized policy forms specified by individual states. Most states, however, now follow the forms designed by the National Association of Insurance Commissioners (NAIC) or by a leading state, such as New York.

An example of mandated standardized measurement and presentation of the terms of financial products is the annual percentage rate of interest (APR) on loans that is required by the 1968 Truth in Lending Act. Although this standardized disclosure may have benefited some borrowers, it has been the source of a large amount of litigation and has imposed costs on lenders and on borrowers who repay their obligations. The major reason for the litigation and the attendant costs is that some borrowers who default on their loans have an incentive to claim that the interest rate as stated violates the act. If they can show that a requirement of the act was violated, even if only technically, they are relieved of their debt, and the lender must pay their legal costs. A class action suit brought on behalf of a large number of similar borrowers can be very expensive for lenders. As a result, a large body of very detailed rulings specifying how interest rates should be calculated and presented has been produced by the Federal Reserve Board (which is charged with administering the law) in response to inquiries by banks trying to avoid lawsuits.[32] It is not clear whether, on balance, the law has resulted in a net benefit to consumers as a group or has simply added to the costs of lending, which are passed on to borrowers.

**Enhanced Consumer Confidence.** Below I examine consumer confidence in three areas: banks, securities firms and equities markets, and insurance companies.

*Consumer confidence in banks.* Government-provided deposit insurance has certainly increased consumer confidence in the safety of their deposits. This provides a net benefit to banks and other depository institutions to the extent that the full cost of deposit insurance is not charged to them, but rather is absorbed by taxpayers. It is the taxpayers who are responsible for the contingent risk that the fund or ex post charges to banks will be insufficient to cover the loss, as happened when the Federal Savings and Loan Insurance Corporation went bankrupt.

*Consumer confidence in securities firms and equities markets.* Securities firms also benefit when consumers believe they do not have to incur the cost of investigating the solvency of these firms, since they are protected by a government agency. The Securities Investor Protection Insurance Corporation (SIPIC) guarantees the accounts of investors held by securities firms from fraud and insolvency losses of up to $500,000 per account, although not as a result of changes in the market values of securities. Perhaps because there have been very few failures of securities firms that resulted in such losses to investors, there is no evidence that this protection has or has not played much of a role in investors' interest in purchasing and owning equity securities.

Two pieces of legislation have been credited with encouraging people's participation in the securities market: the Securities Act of 1933, which regulates the information that must be disclosed to investors in new securities issues, and the Securities and Exchange Act of 1934, which regulates periodic disclosure of financial information by corporations with publicly owned equities. But the evidence does not support this accreditation; indeed, the contrary appears to have occurred. The Securities Act of 1933 substantially increased the cost of a prospectus and the potential liability from lawsuits against issuers and their attorneys and accountants. Consequently, even accounting for the negative effects of the 1930s depression and changes in the price level, the amount of net equity issues (net of redemptions to adjust for issues floated merely for refinancing) in the following five years declined substantially as compared with issues before passage of the act.[33] Although the ratio of net equity issues to capital expenditures increased after World War II until 1953, the last year of the study cited (Benston 1969), it did not reach the pre-1933 levels.

Furthermore, the conservative accounting disclosure requirements imposed by the SEC appear to have driven a substantial proportion of bond and equity issues out of the public market and into the private placement market, which is not subject to those requirements. This was particularly the case for firms that found it difficult to inform the public of their prospects, because they were not permitted to include projections and estimates in their financial reports (Benston 1969, 67–73.) The possible benefits of the Securities Act of 1933 were studied by Gregg Jarrell (1981), who examined the returns to stockholders from new issues before and after passage of the legislation, adjusted for market returns. He found no improvement in returns. Risk, though, did decrease. The reduction appears to be the result of screening out more risky issues, which means that some particularly profitable as well as unprofitable ventures were not started, and of a shift of some riskier bonds to private placements.

The Securities and Exchange Act of 1934 has also imposed considerable costs on corporations and their owners, in the form of higher information production costs, accounting and legal fees, and restricted ability to communicate with potential investors. The benefits, however, are not evident. I measured potential benefits to investors by examining the changes from February 1934 through December 1935 in the share prices of the 62 percent of New York Stock Exchange–traded corporations that previously disclosed their sales (turnover) and the remaining 38 percent that had to report sales for the first time (Benston 1973a). The share prices of both groups were adjusted for contemporaneous changes in the stock market in general. The analysis clearly shows that changes in the share prices of both groups over that period were almost identical. Changes in the risk of the shares were in fact greater for the companies that had been disclosing sales. These results are inconsistent with the belief that government-required disclosure provided investors with useful information.

The effect and effectiveness of mandated disclosure has been further studied in a very large number of papers. Many of these are reviewed and summarized in Gonedes and Dopuch (1974), Benston (1976, 123–36), Benston (1979), Lev and Ohlson (1982), Bernard (1989), and Cho and Jung (1991). Most of these studies examine the effect of announcements of earnings on the prices of portfolios of stocks. They do not distinguish between numbers that were disclosed voluntarily and those that were disclosed because of an SEC or Financial Accounting Standards Board (FASB) mandate. They generally find a relatively small effect on stock prices.

The few studies that examine mandated disclosure—such as income and expense by line of business, price level–adjusted data, replacement-cost data, oil- and gas-exploration expenditures, lease capitalization, pension liabilities, foreign currency translations, use of generally accepted accounting principles by banks, restatement of investments in securities to market values, and disclosure of fully diluted earnings per share—have found either no effect or small effects on stock prices. Thus it appears that mandated disclosure has added little information that was not already incorporated in stock prices, or was of little or no value to investors.

It should therefore not be surprising that the interest by potential investors in purchasing and trading equities has not been noticeably affected by government-mandated financial-disclosure requirements. This is clear from the substantial increases and decreases in stock market activity in the United States, the United Kingdom, and other countries that are unrelated to the degree of mandated disclosure. Indeed, it appears that disclosure by publicly traded corporations follows rather than leads investor interest and is motivated by the desire on the part of corporations to sell their securities to a wider public. An analysis of corporate financial disclosure in the United Kingdom as compared with the United States indicates that its extent can be reasonably explained by the extent of ownership of corporate shares (Benston 1975a, 251–54).

*Consumer confidence in insurance companies.* Government supervision of insurance companies probably has increased the confidence of consumers, who have come to believe that the beneficiaries of their policies will be paid what is due to them. There are two particularly important factors: consumer confidence that the companies will be able and will be willing to pay claims filed. Meier (1988, chapter 4) describes periods in the nineteenth and early-through-mid-twentieth centuries when insurance companies regularly became insolvent and wrote policies with fine print and abstruse clauses that excluded many claims. He does not indicate whether or how the regulatory reforms dealing with the operations, solvency, and trade practices of insurance companies enacted in the early twentieth century increased consumers' willingness to purchase insurance.

Although a required capital standard enforced by field examinations may have made some insurance companies less prone to failure, it does not appear to be a binding restraint for most U.S. companies. In 1992, only 2.0 percent of property-liability insurers and 1.7 percent of life-health insurers had capital below the NAIC-formula risk-based amount, while 91.8 and 92.4 percent of the companies had capital exceeding 250 percent of the risk-based amount (Klein 1995, table 3). Rather, it appears that market forces are a more important determinant of capital, with potential customers relying on such private rating services as A. M. Best.[34]

*Conclusions on consumer confidence.* Consumer confidence in financial institutions—banks, securities companies, and insurance companies—appears to be greater because they are supervised by government agencies. This is a benefit for both financial-product producers and consumers. The costs of the supervision, however, are not obvious to consumers (or, at times, taxpayers), who ultimately pay for it. These costs include maintaining the supervisory agencies and the costs they impose on producers. In the United States the cost of supervision is particularly heavy for banks and insurance companies, which are subject to field examinations, and for corporations that must comply with the SEC's mandated financial-disclosure requirements.

Probably the greatest cost to consumers comes from regulatory restraints on competition. Regulation often prohibits firms from offering products that might compete with those offered by regulated financial-services firms, and it restricts these firms from competing with each other. As is shown next, this benefit to regulated financial-services firms explains, in large measure, why their regulation continues despite its costs and its general paucity of other economic benefits.

**Protection from Competition by Alternative Sources of Financial Services.** Demands by producers of financial services for regulations that protect them from competition is the final, and perhaps the most important, reason why these regulations were enacted and are maintained. Two aspects of such protection are market entry and restrictions on deposit-interest payments.

*Entry into markets and products.* As was described earlier at the beginning of this chapter, entry into banking markets was restricted by governments to increase their revenue from seigniorage, to obtain gains for monarchs and their supporters from low- or no-interest (and, at times, no-repayment) loans and from partial ownership of protected banks. In the United States, bank charters were granted by legislators, who could obtain payment from applicants and act on their behalf to restrict new charters, and who required banks to purchase government bonds. U.S. legislators have also restricted mergers among banks and have not permitted banks to establish nationwide branches or even (in some states) intrastate branches, in response to populist fears about the power that might be wielded by very big banks.

Although restraints on potentially dominant banks (particularly those headquartered in money centers) were often given as the principal reason for prohibiting both inter- and intrastate branching in the United States, these restrictions were enacted largely to curtail competition among banks. Indeed, the successful competition of the First and Second Banks of the United States with state-chartered banks resulted in their twenty-year charters' not being renewed by Congress. In addition, states limited or prohibited branching within their borders and across state lines to protect smaller banks from competition from larger, state-chartered banks that might establish branches in their areas. Presumably, large branch banks would achieve such great economies of scale or political power that a single or a few banks would dominate banking, if banks were permitted to expand and branch without limit.

This argument lost whatever validity it might have had when the United States adopted the Sherman Antitrust Act in 1890. Furthermore, the experience of states that did not constrain intrastate branching, particularly California, showed that not only large banks developed and prospered: so did smaller and medium-sized ones. When the legislatures of states with restrictive branching laws relaxed those laws, the legislatures tended to permit entry into previously protected markets only via purchase of existing banks. Restrictions on interstate branching were removed only when it became clear that technology had eroded the previously protected banks' advantages.

Expressed concerns about safety and soundness have supported restrictions on the activities that banks could undertake. These restrictions, described in chapter 1, have served predominantly to constrain competition by and from banks and other companies and among banks, particularly in the United States. In practice, the restrictions have tended to make commercial banks more rather than less prone to failure, since they have reduced the banks' ability to diversify their activities.[35]

The legal separation of commercial and investment banking in the United States, enacted in the Banking Act of 1933 (the Glass-Steagall Act), is perhaps the most severe restriction imposed on U.S. commercial banks, particularly now that restrictions on branching are being removed. Several justifications have been given for this separation, which is unique among nations except for Japan, forced to adopt U.S. laws after World War II. These include allegations that losses from banks' securities operations were responsible for many failures during the Great Depression; that smaller banks failed because larger banks "pushed" them into purchasing debt obligations that defaulted; and that commercial banks suffered from inherent conflicts of interest in their positions as depositories and as securities' underwriters and brokers.

I examined each of these (and other) charges in Benston (1990). In fact, banks that engaged in securities activities had lower rates of failure than had otherwise similar banks that did not. The failures of smaller banks were rarely the result of losses on securities; losses on loans, then as now, are the principal reason for failures. I also examined each of the charges made in congressional hearings and by later commentators that commercial banks had conflicts of interest in their roles as both depositories and securities underwriters and dealers, and that they had engaged in securities-related actions to the detriment of consumers. These allegations included getting depositors and trusts to take overpriced securities that the banks had underwritten, misstating prospectuses, and repaying bank loans that might default with the proceeds from bank-underwritten securities. None of these or other charges have any basis in fact (Benston 1990, chapter 4).

The Banking Act of 1933 and other legislation adopted in the United States as a consequence of the Great Depression provide an excellent example of the use of regulation to restrict competition. The Franklin Roosevelt administration sought legislation that would control the "excesses" of the securities market, which it blamed in part for the Great Depression. The Securities Act of 1933 and the Securities and Exchange Act of 1934 served this purpose. This legislation benefited investment bankers, who preferred a single federal law to the multiple state-enacted Blue Sky laws that governed new issues of securities. Investment bankers also wanted commercial banks removed from competition for underwriting, as there was little business to go around and the banks had rapidly been increasing their share of the market.

Most of the commercial banks that were involved in underwriting were willing to leave the field (especially Chase National Bank, but not National City Bank), both because they wanted to reduce their payrolls and because they realized that they would have to pay some price for their (incorrectly) presumed responsibility for the depression. In addition, the banks were not adversely affected by the Securities and Exchange Act of 1934, from which they were exempted because they were already regulated.

Small banks did not want restrictions on branching removed, and they had reason to fear that their depositors would shift their funds to the large branch banks, almost none of which had failed. Indeed, the failures were concentrated among small banks located in small towns that could have been served by branches of larger banks (Benston 1973b). Consequently, small banks wanted deposit insurance. They did not have to pay much for the insurance, however. The assessments were paid substantially by the large banks (which had large-dollar deposit accounts), because assessments were made on total deposits, even though only the first $2,500 per account was covered (raised to $5,000 in 1934). The large banks were willing to pay for deposit insurance because the Banking Act of 1933 prohibited the payment of interest on demand deposits—a benefit the banks had been unable to obtain earlier, because the antitrust laws prevented them from enforcing previously attempted cartel agreements.

The large banks' savings of deposit interest almost exactly offset the cost to them of deposit insurance (Golembe 1975). In addition, weak banks were closed and it became almost impossible for anyone to get a bank charter or small-loan license, as applicants had to show that an additional institution was necessary to meet potential customers' "convenience and needs." Thus, the existing financial institutions got what they wanted under the guise of enhancing safety, and consumers did not recognize the cost to them of restricted competition.

*Restrictions on deposit-interest payments.* Because only banks are permitted to offer the very valuable service of transfer of funds by check or deposit-account entry, they would benefit as a group if they could restrict the amount of interest paid to depositors. In the United Kingdom, which had relatively few large banks, such restrictions could be agreed to and enforced with cartel-like understandings. Such agreements have been illegal in the United States since 1890. Furthermore, the greater number of banks made it difficult for large, money-center banks to reach and maintain such an understanding.

The crisis of the Great Depression presented them with the opportunity of having the government enforce a ban on demand-deposit interest payments. It has been alleged that the prohibition of interest on demand deposits enacted in the Banking Act of 1933 was necessary to prevent banks from engaging in destructive competition, which presumably led them into making risky loans that (at least in the short run) they funded with deposits attracted by higher rates of interest. I examined this issue and found that banks that paid interest tended to be located in more competitive markets, both for deposits and for loans (Benston 1964). They did not make riskier loans and had lower rates of failure than banks that paid little or no explicit interest on demand deposits. When the Great Depression hit, banks that paid for deposits with interest rather than with services were able to reduce their costs more quickly and, as a result, had a better chance of surviving.

The Banking Act of 1933 also empowered the Federal Reserve to establish a ceiling on interest rates for commercial banks' time deposits, apparently because legislators feared that deposit insurance might permit risk-prone banks to bid wildly for deposits. A similar ceiling was not imposed on savings and loan associations (S&Ls), in part because the insurance on those institutions' deposits (which, at that time, were equity shares) was restricted, unlike FDIC insurance. "Depositors" in failed S&Ls were repaid as funds became available. The ceiling on bank savings deposits was set above the market rate of interest; hence, it was not binding, until the inflation of the late 1960s resulted in nominal interest rates' exceeding the ceiling. At that time, S&Ls increasingly bid for savings funds. The ceiling was then extended to S&Ls, to protect them and banks from having to compete for depositors' funds; but it was set slightly higher for S&Ls, to encourage fund flows into residential mortgages.

Market-interest rates declined in the early 1970s and then increased again in the late 1970s, as a result of the sharp increases in oil prices and the Federal Reserve's inflation of the money supply. The ceiling continued to be binding, until it became clear in 1980 that technological and other developments had made it feasible for savers to withdraw their funds and obtain higher, market-determined rates of interest by investing in money market mutual funds and other investments paying market rates of interest. MMMFs sold investors shares of U.S. Treasury bills and notes and bank-issued $100,000 certificates of deposit (CDs) that were permitted to pay market rates of interest. These funds grew from $3.7 billion at year-end 1977 to $206.6 billion at year-end 1982. From 1980 through 1986, to stem the outflow of funds from banks and S&Ls, interest-rate ceilings on time and savings deposits were gradually removed.[36]

**Conclusions—Benefits to Regulated Financial Institutions.** Regulation could help financial institutions standardize those aspects of their operations that are mutually dependent, such as check-clearance symbols for banks, financial reports for banks and insurance companies, and financial reports for companies with publicly traded stock. There is little evidence, however, to suggest that standardization agreements could not be and were not developed by financial institutions and investors without the aid of government agencies in the absence of regulation.

Some government-required information could be helpful to consumers: for example, basic, audited financial statements; data on payments to corporate promoters and insiders; and key terms on insurance policies. Standardized, required reporting of fees and costs charged to consumers of financial products can also help efficient firms and potential new entrants inform consumers about the benefits of their products as compared with alternatives. But mandated disclosure becomes very detailed and costly to produce and verify. Furthermore, it may not actually be relevant to the requirements of many or even most consumers, and data requirements tend to expand. The cost of these requirements falls more heavily on potential new entrants, and that circumstance reduces competition, to the detriment of consumers. Thus, although mandated disclosure does achieve some benefits for consumers and some producers, on balance it is costly to them.

Consumers usually have more confidence in financial institutions that are regulated. This fact can provide a positive externality, to the extent that people might not otherwise purchase insurance and annuities, thereby putting a greater burden on society.

But the belief that investors have greater confidence in securities markets because publicly traded corporations are required to produce financial statements in accordance with government mandates is not empirically supported. Furthermore, these mandates appear to have constrained the information that corporations might have provided voluntarily to investors, and increased the cost to corporations that want to go public.

The most important benefit of regulation to producers, with concomitant cost to consumers, has been its use to restrict competition. Such restrictions have included restraints on entry, on the products that financial institutions can offer to the public, and on the prices they are permitted to pay for deposits.

# 3

## 𝍇

# *Intended and Unintended Costs of Regulation*

Regulation is usually costly, particularly when government agencies are given a general mandate to keep financial institutions from becoming insolvent or from failing to meet an obligation to produce financial products that are effective and are fairly priced.[37] Two kinds of costs may be distinguished. The "intended costs" of regulation are those that people favoring the legislation on which the regulations are based could reasonably have envisioned. "Unintended costs" are those that the initial supporters and drafters of the legislation probably did not foresee or were willing to discount because the events giving rise to them were considered unlikely to occur or were expected to occur at some distant time.

## Intended Costs

Government agencies charged with regulating financial services must incur direct salary and other operating expenses. These expenses are met from general tax receipts, from fees imposed on the regulated firms, from seigniorage on currency (such as Federal Reserve and Bank of England notes), and (in the United States) from earnings on banks' required reserves in excess of amounts that banks would have voluntarily kept. The regulated firms incur the direct costs of fulfilling regulators' demands for reports and the costs imposed by field examiners and fees charged by the regulatory agencies.

Franks, Schaefer, and Staunton (1997) estimated the annual government-incurred and company-incurred costs of regulating securities and derivatives trading and brokering and investment management in the United Kingdom, the United States, and France, using data from 1991 through 1993. Banking is not included. The data were gathered from reports of the government and self-regulatory agencies and from nine securities firms and thirteen investment management firms.[38] They report aggregate agency-incurred (direct) costs of £67.7 million ($99.5 million at the then exchange rate of $1.47 = £1) in the United Kingdom and £401.2 million ($589.7 million) in the United States. Compliance costs that the companies surveyed (presumably in the United Kingdom) claimed would not have been incurred if they were not regulated, extrapolated to an industry total, are £149–191 million ($219–281 million) for securities firms and £35–36 million ($51–53 million) for investment-management firms.

The indirect costs of regulation, which are not estimated by Franks, Schaefer, and Staunton (1997), are probably larger than the direct costs. One indirect cost is imposed by community activists (in the United States), who force banks and thrifts to make less-than-market-rate loans to groups that the activists believe are deserving in exchange for not blocking or delaying the institutions' requests for regulatory approval of mergers, acquisitions, and branch closures. Another indirect cost for commercial and investment banks and insurance companies in the United States is the prohibition against services their customers might demand, as outlined earlier. This cost is borne by both the consumers and the affected institutions.

It is likely that legislators, regulated institutions, and community activists were aware that the costs of regulation would be substantial. Presumably, they believed that the benefits to them would exceed the costs *they* would have to incur. It is doubtful that they took into account the costs that others—producers and other consumers—would have to pay. As was discussed earlier, it is likely that the costs to consumers, who ultimately pay the costs imposed on producers, and to taxpayers exceed the benefits they receive.

## Unintended Costs

The unintended costs of regulation include: (1) instability of the financial system because financial institutions are prohibited from diversifying their activities effectively; (2) costs that have escalated beyond the level originally intended; (3) costs to financial institutions of regulations that were once beneficial to them, but now primarily increase their costs and prevent them from serving their customers effectively; and (4) the costs to consumers and the economy from the absence of less costly products, because some suppliers were prevented from competing with established firms.

**Banking System Instability.** Particularly in the United States, financial institutions have had to hold overly risky asset positions and engage in overly specialized activities that were legally mandated.[39] Most recently, mandated specialization was the principal cause of the more than $150 billion present-value cost to taxpayers as a result of the S&L and savings-bank failures of the 1980s. These thrifts were required to hold long-term, fixed-interest-rate mortgages that were funded with short-term, government-insured liabilities—savings and time accounts. Had it not been for deposit insurance, it is doubtful that people would have entrusted their funds to such institutions, or that these institutions would have been organized by entrepreneurs. Indeed, before 1934, S&Ls were funded predominantly with equity shares. Deposit insurance was extended to S&L shares in 1934 to help the home building industry. As long as interest rates were stable, the industry could prosper by lending long and borrowing short. When market-interest rates increased sharply in 1979–1981, the economic value of the thrifts' fixed-interest mortgage loans decreased, resulting in the insolvency of approximately three-quarters of the industry (Benston and Kaufman 1990). Rather than admit that the Federal Savings and Loan Insurance Corporation (FSLIC, which insured S&L deposits) was insolvent, the industry's regulatory agency, the Federal Home Loan Bank

Board (FHLBB), permitted economically insolvent institutions (called "zombies") to continue operations.

The FHLBB was able to forbear from closing economically insolvent S&Ls because *failure* is defined officially in terms of book (historical cost) rather than market value, and capital losses resulting from interest-rate changes are not recognized by traditional accounting until the assets are disposed of (realized) or written off the books. As conditions worsened, the FHLBB reduced S&Ls' capital requirements and permitted them to increase the amount of book-value equity with "regulatory" accounting procedures that delayed the recording of losses. The FHLBB also encouraged S&Ls to expand and attempt to "grow out" of their troubles. Finally, in 1981 S&Ls were permitted to offer variable-interest-rate mortgages, and in 1982 they were permitted to invest in shorter-term assets, including consumer and commercial loans and a greater proportion of commercial real estate loans, to reduce their duration mismatch. Although many S&Ls incurred large losses as a consequence of having made commercial real estate loans that went bad, approximately three-quarters of the losses and most of the failures were the result of the 1979–1981 rise in interest rates (Benston and Carhill 1994).

Deregulation of deposit-interest rates in 1980 did not cause the thrift institutions' losses. On the contrary, removal of ceilings on deposit interest rates allowed S&Ls to retain funds that depositors would have moved to such higher-paying assets as money market mutual funds (MMMFs). Deregulation at least allowed many S&Ls to survive long enough to benefit from the decline in interest rates after 1981, although the 1982 Garn-St Germain Act did permit some S&Ls to make poorly and occasionally improperly written commercial real estate loans.[40] But, had these S&Ls been required to hold higher levels of capital, most of them could have survived the losses.[41] Furthermore, had the thrifts been permitted to invest in more diversified portfolios of assets and to offer variable-interest-rate mortgages, they would not have been as badly damaged by the 1979–1981 increase in market-interest rates.

The U.S. bank failures of the 1980s can be ascribed in large measure to two regulation-driven factors. One is their low levels of capital, which deposit insurance permitted (indeed, encouraged) them to hold. The other is their holding underdiversified asset portfolios, in part a consequence of laws restricting branching and products, particularly securities and insurance brokerage and underwriting.

A less recent, but much more devastating, example is the failure of more than 9,000 banks in the United States during the 1930s Great Depression. As was noted earlier, state laws prohibited interstate branching, and many states prohibited or restricted intrastate branching. The Banking Act of 1864, which established federal chartering of banks, was interpreted as allowing national banks to operate out of only one office. (Later legislation permitted national banks to branch to the same extent as state-chartered banks.) When, in the early 1930s, the Federal Reserve permitted the nation's money supply to decline by approximately a third by failing to counteract runs to gold and currency, some 40 percent of U.S. banks failed. But, as noted earlier, the overwhelming number of failures occurred among small-unit banks located in small towns; almost no branch banks failed. Nor did any banks in Canada (which permitted nationwide branching) close, although they may have been economically insolvent.

Deposit insurance has had diametrically opposite effects on banking stability. It has increased stability by removing the incentive of insured depositors to run from banks they believe might be or become insolvent. As noted earlier, however, this need not be a problem if the central bank maintains the money supply. In contrast, as noted earlier, deposit insurance has *decreased* stability by permitting and encouraging banks and thrifts to increase their portfolio risk and to hold lower amounts of capital, which makes them more vulnerable to losses. (Further discussion of the importance of this source of instability is deferred to chapter 4.)

**Escalating Costs of Regulation.** Goodhart et al. (1998, chapter 4) cogently express the tendency of regulation to expand substantially. They point out that because consumers do not pay explicitly for regulation, it is seen as a "free" good. Hence, they say, "this non-price administrative mechanism has an in-built tendency towards providing an 'excessive' amount of regulation, so that the burden (costs at the margin) of regulatory compliance can exceed the benefits." As is discussed in chapter 2, existing producers of financial services also demand regulation as a means of restricting competitors.

Legislators tend to serve constituents who demand restrictive legislation and regulations, because these beneficiaries of regulation are better organized to influence and financially support legislators than are consumers or potential competitive suppliers. In addition, legislators tend to favor such legislation—the greater the extent of regulation, the greater the possibilities for serving and doing favors for regulated firms in return for campaign contributions.[42]

The staffs and leadership of regulatory agencies also extend the reach and depth of regulations. In part, they do this to satisfy the firms they are charged with regulating. This tendency is enhanced by the regulators' regular contact with the regulated firms, rather than with consumers and unregulated firms, and by a "revolving door," whereby professionals move from and to regulated firms and regulatory agencies. Thus the regulators are "captured" by the regulated.[43]

Whether or not they are captured, regulators benefit from extending their budgets and bureaucracies (Downs 1967). They also face asymmetric rewards and punishment that discourage them from reducing the burden of the regulations they administer. Consider what might happen if they reduce the scope and intensity of regulation because they believe that the regulatory costs exceed the benefits to consumers—and their expectation is fulfilled. If the benefits or costs to consumers are not obvious ("salient," in the jargon of political scientists), as is often the case, because the relationship between regulatory costs and prices paid by consumers is unclear, the regulators will get little credit. Nor would they be thanked by firms that are now permitted to offer new products, because these firms would probably (and reasonably) believe that they succeeded because of their efforts and genius rather than as a result of the regulators' sufferance. The regulators (and legislators), however, will face criticism from regulated firms that face more competition. As a result, regulators and legislators are likely to get less support from their constituents and are less likely to obtain well-paying jobs in the regulated firms when they decide to leave government service.

Conversely, if the regulators' expectation of net benefits to consumers is not fulfilled, they will be criticized. Worse yet, there might be a crisis or disaster that they will be blamed for having allowed to happen or failed to prevent. For example, when the Continental Illinois Bank had absorbed substantial losses from bad loans that drove it into insolvency in 1984, federal regulators could have closed the bank and made depositors with accounts of more than $100,000 assume a share of the costs proportionate to their uninsured deposits. The regulators feared, however, that if this were done, depositors with balances of more than $100,000 would run from some other, presumably weak, large banks. Although these funds would still remain in the banking system, some large banks might fail, giving the appearance of a banking crisis.

Additionally, many banks had deposits with Continental; the authorities feared that the losses borne by these banks would endanger their solvency. Alternatively, large depositors might have distinguished between Continental and other banks and not run (as Benston et al. [1986] found), and the losses imposed on other banks would not have been large enough to render them insolvent (as Kaufman [1996] has shown). Furthermore, bailing out Continental's large depositors would be costly in the future; if similar, presumably sophisticated people and firms came to believe that all depositors would be bailed out, they would no longer have to be concerned about the safety of their banks. Although the benefits from imposing costs on uninsured depositors appear much greater than the costs of not doing so, the regulators guaranteed all of Continental's and its holding company's liabilities. From their short-run viewpoint, this was a sensible action.

Regulators also are likely to be criticized should they forbear from extending the scope of regulations when this might have benefited an interested party or might be portrayed as having prevented a disaster from happening. For example, in 1985 the Bank of England guaranteed the holders of deposits with Johnson-Matthey Bankers Limited, a separately capitalized unit of a firm that specialized in gold and other precious metals. The justification for this bailout was that if it were not done, investors would lose confidence in similar UK firms. The history of increasingly expansive requirements adopted by the U.S. Securities and Exchange Commission, as documented in Benston (1976, chapter

3 and chapter 5, section 5.3), provides another, more extensive example of "regulatory creep." In response to complaints that may have affected only a few companies, the SEC has extended its disclosure requirements to all registered corporations.

At times the extension of regulations and regulatory oversight appears justified. In these instances, regulators are likely to extend the regulations, even though the benefits from possibly solving a problem are greatly exceeded by the costs imposed on all corporations over a long period (since regulations are rarely rescinded, even after they have outlived their usefulness). For example, despite the fact that the Securities and Exchange Act of 1934 simply called for disclosure, the SEC subsequently would not permit corporations to report estimated values of assets (such as the value of petroleum reserves) and disclose that the numbers were estimates, because the values could not readily be verified and, in some instances, had been grossly inflated. Consequently, even when such estimates would have been much more useful to investors than historical costs, publicly traded corporations have been prohibited from disclosing them.

Currently, following large losses incurred by a few corporations from trading in derivatives, the SEC has required all corporations to disclose a wealth of detail about their derivatives holdings and transactions, including those used to hedge risks. Apparently the SEC did not consider whether the total cost to all registered corporations of preparing and presenting this information was likely to exceed the benefit to investors from obtaining the information. Nor does the SEC appear concerned about the cost to investors of firms having to inform competitors of corporate strategy, or of avoiding the use of derivatives as hedges.

Regulatory creep is often driven by nongovernment people. They believe that the regulations either should be expanded to cover something they consider important (such as reporting in financial statements the monetary cost of environmental degradation presumably inflicted by a corporation, or data on transactions in and holdings of derivatives), or should include information from which they hope to profit. Experience with the 1968 Truth-in-Lending (TIL) Act provides a good example of the latter. The act appears to be laudable, in that it simply requires disclosure of a standard measure of the annual percentage interest rate (APR) that borrowers will be asked to pay. The Senate Report states:

> The basic purpose of the Truth-in-Lending bill is to pro-
> vide a *full disclosure* of credit charges to the American
> consumer. The bill does not in any way regulate the
> credit industry nor does it prescribe ceilings on credit
> charges. Instead it requires that *full disclosure* of credit
> charges be made so that the consumer can deduce for
> himself whether the charge is reasonable. [cited by Dur-
> kin and Elliehausen, 1990, p. 258, emphasis added]

Although the full-disclosure requirement may appear to be unambiguously beneficial (more is better than less) or, at worst,
innocuous, the TIL Act has proved to be very costly. It has been
interpreted to include all information that might conceivably be
useful to someone at some time. Furthermore, it is unclear
whether charges, such as mailing fees and lien-recording fees,
should be included in the calculation of the APR. (Indeed, a class
action suit against banks in Florida charged that they had misled mortgagors by not including a Federal Express charge in the
APR; hence, the mortgagors owed nothing. The plaintiffs prevailed in court and it took an act of Congress to reverse the decision.)

To protect themselves against lawsuits, banks have re-
quested rulings from the Federal Reserve, which was given
responsibility for administering the act, on almost every conceiv-
able loan, and they have petitioned the Congress for changes. By
1990 the act had been amended twelve times. It had grown to 32
pages from the original 13, and the regulations included 211
pages of official interpretation. Nevertheless, many thousands of
court cases were filed in federal courts. It is not known whether
consumers have benefited from the act. Durkin and Elliehausen
(1990, 264) surveyed the literature on the potential benefits
achieved by the act, and report that "survey data indicate that
consumer awareness of credit costs has increased since implementation of TIL . . . [although there has been] little change in
credit shopping by consumers." They could not find any studies
of the effect of the act on the cost of credit.

**Costly and Restrictive Regulations Borne by Present Sup-
pliers.** As was discussed in chapter 2, banks and other financial

institutions benefited from regulations that restricted entry into their markets and reduced competition among themselves. Over time, as other suppliers' incentives to obtain funds from consumers grew as a result of increases in the nominal rate of interest, and as technology improved and the cost of serving consumers decreased, the benefits from restrictive regulations decreased.

These changes are most striking in the United States, which has imposed a higher degree of regulation on financial institutions than has the United Kingdom. The benefits some banks enjoyed from restrictions on branching were reduced as inflation drove nominal interest rates above the regulatory ceilings, which induced savers to put their funds in money market mutual funds. Business firms developed money management programs to reduce their deposits practically to zero, and competition drove banks to offer "sweep accounts," wherein balances on which interest could not be paid were transferred to interest-bearing deposits or obligations. Branching restrictions were further eroded as automatic teller machines (ATMs) made it possible for people to withdraw and deposit funds in many locations. (Lending and other banking services were not restrained by antibranching laws.) It is probably for these reasons that state legislators offered reciprocal holding company privileges to banks in adjacent states and Congress enacted legislation in 1994 that now permits nationwide branching, except for states that "opt out."

The separation of investment and commercial banking mandated by the Glass-Steagall Act is being eroded as banks find ways to offer these services and as investment banks and securities firms find ways to offer the equivalent of checking accounts. The federal regulatory authorities (particularly the Comptroller of the Currency, who supervises nationally chartered banks) have increasingly interpreted the law liberally. I believe that these changes have occurred because the formerly protected institutions have come to realize that there was not much left to protect. They might also be looking forward to being bought out now at substantial premiums by institutions that want to enter their previously restricted markets.

As electronic fund transfers become first economically feasible and then economically desirable, and as sales of securities, mutual funds, and insurance via the Internet are developed and become more acceptable to consumers, financial-services firms might have to change their delivery procedures and products to compete successfully. It is doubtful whether they can do this under the present system of financial services regulation. Hence, although some firms might still benefit from the present regulatory structure, the benefits to most firms are soon likely to disappear.

**Restraints on New Entrants.** A possibly unintended effect of regulation is to restrict, if not bar, the entry of new firms and products. In part this is a consequence of regulatory capture. To some extent the cost to existing firms is lower because they have incurred the fixed cost of producing in a regulated environment. Hence, the variable cost to them of meeting the requirements is lower than the cost new entrants would have to incur, which gives existing firms a cost advantage over potential rivals. The managers of existing firms may also have prospered, more because they know how to work with regulators and regulations than because of other skills, such as determining consumer demand and developing new and better products.

Thus, one consequence of the regulatory situation for consumers is that they have a lesser possibility of being offered better alternatives. The economy generally suffers for the same reason. It is true that new products are often developed to avoid the regulations (such as interest-bearing negotiable orders of withdrawal [NOW] transactions accounts) or to deal with situations engendered by regulations (such as interest-rate futures and options and mortgage-backed obligations that serve to offset the duration risk faced by specialized S&Ls). But the cost of developing these products might have been avoided or have been lower, had the regulations not existed.

Once alternatives have been developed and are accepted by consumers, the regulatory advantage to existing suppliers is eroded. An example is money market mutual funds. Although these funds prospered because they offered consumers close-to-market rates of interest when interest-rate ceilings were binding, after the interest-rate ceilings were removed from banks and thrifts the MMMFs continued to be used by consumers, even though the funds are not insured by a government agency.

## Conclusions on the Cost of Regulation

Regulation has been and continues to be costly to consumers. Some of these costs may be justified, if the regulations serve to reduce negative externalities sufficiently. Some regulations also might be cost effective for protecting consumers against unfair market practices. Although the regulations generally have benefited many producers of financial services (at the expense of consumers), over time their value for this purpose has eroded, while the cost has increased. Hence, a change in the present situation might be politically feasible.

Chapter 4 now describes an alternative structure that, if adopted, would benefit consumers, taxpayers, and most producers.

# 4

## Optimal Regulation of Financial Services

From the analysis presented earlier, I conclude that regulation of financial services and financial-services firms that is beneficial to consumers and taxpayers is justified only to the extent that it reduces or eliminates the cost of negative externalities in:

- de jure or de facto government-provided deposit insurance, because experience indicates that governments cannot avoid bailing out depositors, and the public will not accept privately provided deposit insurance, as was discussed in chapter 2
- government-mandated, third-party liability insurance
- lower-than-optimal use of life insurance and annuities, because of policyholders' difficulties in monitoring insurance companies

In addition, some form of government regulation could be effective for:

- monitoring banks' and insurance companies' solvency in place of monitoring by consumers with relatively small deposit accounts and policies (assuming this is more cost effective than monitoring by consumers)

• protecting consumers from fraud, unfair dealing, and invidious discrimination

The optimal regulatory system explained below entails, first, a capital requirement for banks and insurance companies that would virtually eliminate the negative externalities and save depositors and consumers of the specified insurance products the cost of evaluating and monitoring the solvency of their institutions. The proposed system imposes very low costs on financial institutions, consumers, and taxpayers. As is explained below, it does not include government-determined adjustments for the risks posed by depositories and insurance companies. Nor, as is explained subsequently, is it necessary or desirable to harmonize the regulations or regulatory system of one country with those of other countries, although cooperation among regulators to discourage fraud and tax evasion would be useful.

Second, consumers would be additionally protected by an office that would act as an ombudsman, rather than by direct regulation of financial institutions and markets, as described in the fifth subsection. An overall conclusion is presented at the end of this chapter.

## Deposits and Depository Institutions

The essence of the proposed system is a capital requirement, which is necessary because government-provided deposit insurance removes the incentive for most depositors to monitor the activities of deposit providers (see chapter 2). The amount of capital should be sufficient to absorb almost all losses that might otherwise be charged to depositors. In addition, the capital requirement should:

• not be costly to prudently run depository institutions (hereafter, banks), relative to their costs in a non-deposit-insurance environment
• be easy for the banking authorities to administer
• provide the authorities with a means to deal flexibly with deteriorating situations
• prevent the authorities from forbearing to take necessary actions, so that managers whose banks are in financial difficulties do not believe that they can forestall the authorities' actions

As a result, very little will have to be paid to bail out depositors, and very little supervision and almost no regulation of banks will be necessary. Furthermore, technological changes in the delivery of depository and fund transfer services will be made possible by an alternative to the proposed capital requirement—collateralized deposits.

This proposed basic regulatory system for banks has three parts: (1) a substantial capital requirement that can be met at no higher cost of capital than is faced by unregulated firms; (2) periodic reports of assets, liabilities, and capital to the authorities, preferably measured at economic market values and subject to rules designed to ensure that the capital is "real," attested to by independent public accountants; and (3) structured early intervention and resolution (SEIR) that employs prespecified tripwires or tranches to determine when and how the authorities first may and then must intervene and, if necessary, take over a capital-deficient depository. This system was first proposed in Benston and Kaufman (1988), was elaborated on in Benston et al. (1989), and was adopted in a modified and weakened version in the FDIC Improvement Act of 1991 (FDICIA).[44]

**Capital Requirement**. From the relative amount of capital held by financial institutions in the years before deposit insurance and from the capital held by financial companies with uninsured liabilities,[45] it appears that a requirement of about 15–20 percent of total on- and off-balance-sheet assets would now be adequate.[46] This percentage should be the equivalent of the relative amount that similar financial institutions would hold if none of their debt were insured, implicitly or explicitly, by the government. It is higher than the amount that was held by banks before deposits were insured, for two reasons. One reason (suggested by George Kaufman) is that, in the past, runs by depositors would or could force the prompt closing of an insolvent bank, an outcome that is much quicker than a legal bankruptcy procedure required for other companies. Consequently, it is likely that a relatively lower proportion of assets would be dissipated before the creditors could assert their claims. Furthermore, unlike many other firms, insolvent banks can be and are likely to be acquired in whole or in part by other banks with relatively little (if any) loss to depositors. At present, with de jure or de facto deposit insurance, runs are no longer available as an efficient means to discipline or close badly managed banks. The second reason is that the potential for large losses appears to have increased. Banks' increased dealing in and holding such risky financial products as derivatives and foreign currencies is one source of such losses. Another facing European banks is the increase in competition as restrictions on entry among European Union (EU) countries have been eliminated (Benink and Benston 1999).

It might appear that the percentage suggested (15–20), which exceeds the percentages presently held by most depository institutions, would be costly to them, because equity capital costs more than debt, which for depositories is primarily in the form of deposits. Deposits are less costly to depositories, to the extent that they are subsidized by underpriced deposit insurance. But this subsidy is not in the interests of consumers and taxpayers; indeed, the purpose of regulation should be to eliminate it. Aside from any subsidy, equity is more costly than debt only because, in most countries, factor payments (returns) to equity holders are not a deductible expense for purposes of computing a corporation's tax liability, while interest paid to debt holders is a deductible expense. Hence, after taxes, debt is on average less costly than equity for all corporate taxpayers—depositories and others. That is one reason why explicitly uninsured debt—debentures subordinated to the claims of all other creditors—should be counted fully as capital. Then depositories, along with other tax-paying enterprises, could hold the proportions of equity and debt that would minimize their taxes, all other things being equal. The subordinated debt would have to be in large denominations, so that unsophisticated savers could not be confused by—or claim they were misled into confusing it with—insured certificates of deposit. To count as capital, the debt would have to include a clause that prohibited the insured depository from repaying it, directly or indirectly, for at least two years, to give the authorities time to take necessary actions.

The other regulatory advantage of subordinated debt is that the interest rate a bank would have to pay on it should reflect the risk of nonrepayment perceived by holders; thus, the interest rate required on newly issued or rolled-over debt is the economic equivalent of risk-adjusted deposit insurance premiums. When outstanding subordinated debt is publicly traded, an increase in the market-determined yield provides the banking authorities with an early warning of solvency problems. Unlike equity, debt holders cannot benefit from risk taking by banks, as they get the down side of risks and not the up side.

It might be argued that small banks would find it difficult to find purchasers of their subordinated debt. Such banks would also find raising equity capital even more difficult, however. They would either have to find investors who were willing to purchase minority interests in often closely held banks or give up control to outsiders. But these banks should be able to find insurance companies, pension funds, or other investors to purchase their uninsured debt, because this is what other corporations have to do. The authorities would get a useful indication of a bank's poor or excessively risky management if it found investors unwilling to risk their funds by purchasing a bank's uninsured debt.

Subordinated debt does have a serious limitation that should be recognized by the banking authorities. The benefits it provides from risk-reflecting interest rates and early warning signals would be limited or lost if equity holders were permitted also to hold subordinated debt, directly or indirectly. (If the price of the subordinated debt were set by independent holders, however, marginal holdings of the debt by equity holders would not pose a problem.)

Another limitation (raised in Llewellyn [1998]) is that "(1) it is not permanently available, and, (2) it cannot be used to write off assets." But these are not problems when the debentures cannot be redeemed before the authorities act to resolve an insolvent bank. Then, the debenture holders "take the hit," thereby protecting depositors and the deposit insurance fund. Should a bank have incurred losses that absorbed its equity capital, however, its subordinated debt holders would become the equity holders. They would then have the same incentives as equity holders to take excessive risks.

With subordinated debt counted fully as capital, banks would be treated almost exactly the same as are corporations generally. The only change they would have to make in their liability structure would be to substitute explicitly uninsured debt with maturity of at least two years for, say, certificates of deposit with the same maturity. Unlike other corporations, however, the remainder of banks' liabilities are guaranteed by a government agency. This guarantee would come into force when the market value of a bank's deposit liabilities exceeded its assets, usually because the bank incurred losses as a result of errors in judgment, deliberate risk taking that did not work out, or simply bad fortune. But once it became insolvent or it appeared as if it would become insolvent, its owners would have a strong incentive to take excessive risks (those that would not be taken if the bank owners absorbed all the cost of bad outcomes). That is why the next step in the system is required.

**Periodic Reports and Rules.** The banking authorities can efficiently monitor a bank's capital and operations from the information provided in its financial statements together with supplementary information. These data would include balance sheets and income statements. The numbers should be transmitted at least monthly for most banks, preferably electronically. The banking authorities can import these numbers into computer programs that compare them with previous reports filed by the bank and with numbers taken from reports filed by other banks. Deviations from expectations can be flagged and exception reports printed for the attention of banking supervisors. This statistical analysis should provide the authorities with early warnings of the financial conditions and activities of banks. At the same time, knowing that their operations are monitored, bank managers are unlikely to undertake activities that will arouse the supervisors' concern.

*Contents of reports—market value accounting and validation.* The specific numbers reported should be taken from those that banks normally keep for their own internal-management purposes. The banking authorities could, however, require additional information, which should alert bank managers that they should also be studying these numbers. In particular, the economic market values of assets and liabilities, rather than historical accounting book values, should be monitored by both management and the banking authorities. These values are readily available for traded securities (including options and futures). Loans, the largest portion of most banks' assets, should be reduced to their net collectible value by the traditional accounting procedures of establishing loan loss reserves. Loans that carry variable interest rates are not subject to much interest-rate risk; fixed-interest-rate loans can be (but, under traditional accounting, are not) restated to their present values. Although the market values of fixed assets, such as buildings and equipment, can rarely be estimated inexpensively or accurately, these are a relatively small portion of banks' assets.

The remaining assets are nontraded securities, such as custom-designed derivatives. Although the values of these derivatives can be estimated with models, they depend on data that are imperfectly measured or that must be assumed. As described in Goodhart et al. (1998, chapter 5), a range of reasonable inputs can produce widely varying values. If derivatives are used to hedge a bank's other risks, however, changes in their market values are offset by changes in the value of the hedged assets or liabilities; hence, in general, the market value of the derivatives need not be obtained.[47] Intangible assets are not and rarely can be measured accurately and are not included in bank assets. Hence, bank capital is likely to be understated, making banks less vulnerable to insolvency. Thus, even if market value accounting were required, banks' reporting requirements should impose little additional cost on them.

*Rules establishing the reality of capital in closely held banks.* Owners of closely held banks might avoid the capital requirement by borrowing from their own bank or from related banks, directly or indirectly.[48] Although most countries prohibit equity holders from borrowing their funds back, Liliana Rojas-Suárez and Stephen Weisbrod (1997, 46–49) show how they could avoid this prohibition with reciprocal borrowing, wherein two unrelated parties (A and B) mutually fund their capital contributions to banks each controls with loans from the other's bank. Assume that party A becomes bankrupt and cannot pay his or her loan at all to bank B. That bank would become insolvent if its capital were less than the amount of the loan. With bank B insolvent, party B might not be able to repay his or her loan to bank A. This, in turn, could result in Bank A becoming insolvent.

This situation could be obviated with some additional rules that have been adopted by many countries. Loans for any purpose should not be made to capital holders and related persons and firms that, together, hold more than a small proportion of a bank's capital (say, 5 percent).[49] Loans to any one borrower or group of related borrowers should not exceed more than a relatively small percentage of a bank's capital (say, 15 percent). These rules, if enforced, would deal effectively with the "capital reality" problem. Enforcement of the rules, however, requires some diligence by the banking authorities. In particular, closely held banks and banks that have rapidly increased their capital should be examined immediately and carefully. The sources of the capital increases should be traced. If it cannot be verified that the funds came from investors who are not direct or indirect borrowers from the bank, the authorities should disallow the inclusion of these amounts in the bank's regulatory capital.

*Audits and examinations.* To ensure that the regularly reported numbers are correct, the banks' annual financial reports should be audited by and attested to by independent chartered (certified) public accountants (CPAs).[50] An audit of monthly reports is not suggested because the cost is likely to exceed the benefits. The auditors, however, would be (and, in the United Kingdom, now are) required to notify the authorities immediately of significant and apparently deliberate reporting "errors" that came to their attention. This requirement should not impose an additional cost on banks, because UK banks are already audited by independent public accountants, as are all larger and many smaller U.S. banks. Closely held and undiversified banks should be monitored more carefully than widely owned and highly diversified banks. Special attention should be paid to loans and investments on which losses could impair a bank's capital.

If the reports indicate that a bank is engaging in what appears to be excessively risky behavior, the authorities can request an explanation from the bank's managers and directors, contact its public accountants, and, if necessary, conduct a field examination. Should the bank have incurred losses that reduce its capital, the authorities first can and then must take actions, as described below.

**Structured Early Intervention and Resolution.** SEIR is designed to overcome an important agency problem—regulators' incentives to forbear from closing weak and insolvent banks and the incentives of the owners of those banks to take high risks in a gamble for recovery. Regulators' incentives to increase the scope of regulations are delineated in chapter 3: the problem arises largely because they are criticized when the banks they regulate fail and often not rewarded for reducing regulated banks' burdens and making entry into their markets less costly. Despite (and sometime because of) regulations that are presumed to reduce the risk of failure, bankers make mistakes, incur unexpected losses, and take risks that turn out badly. But bank regulators are often reluctant to close or substantially intervene in a weakened bank that might fail, for three reasons. First is the criticism that their intervention caused depositors and others to lose confidence in the bank, which caused its later failure (even though this probably would have occurred anyway, with even greater losses). Second is the unfounded fear that the regulators caused people to lose confidence in banks generally, which would have resulted in a financial panic. Third, the regulators might hope that the eventual failure would come after they leave office or move on to "more challenging" assignments.[51]

At the same time, bank owners have strong incentives to keep their banks from being closed. Before the advent of deposit insurance, banks' creditors forced banks to close by withdrawing their deposits. But today only the bank authorities can close banks, and bank owners and their allies can bring pressure on them to forbear from this action. Bank owners can also gamble for recovery by making high-risk investments. Such investments can benefit bank owners even if the expected return is negative, because the owners keep the gain, should it occur, while their losses are limited to their remaining investments in their banks ("heads they win, tails prudently run banks or the taxpayers lose").

These moral-hazard and agency problems can be minimized with tripwires or tranches designated by ratios of capital to assets that specify actions that the banking authorities first may take and then must take as the ratios decline. For example, a bank with a capital/asset ratio of 15 (perhaps 20) percent would be classified as "well capitalized." As long as its ratio is above this level, it would be subject to little, if any, supervision and no constraints unless statistical analysis of its reports or warnings from auditors or others (including market intelligence) indicated behavior that could exhaust its capital. If the bank's capital/asset ratio declined below 15 percent but remained above, perhaps, 10 percent, it would be classified as "inadequately capitalized." The authorities would then tell the bank to submit a business plan specifying how it expected to redress the situation; they could (at their discretion) more closely supervise the bank and impose constraints on its dividend distributions, growth, officers' salaries, and the like. Should the bank's capital/asset ratio fall below the 10 percent tripwire, the bank would be classified as "undercapitalized," and the authorities would have no choice but to take such actions as suspending dividends to stockholders and interest payments to holders of subordinated debt that served as capital, restricting transfers to related corporations, limiting growth, and the like.

When the capital/asset ratio is still positive but as low as, say, 5 percent, the authorities would have to resolve (take over) the bank. It is doubtful, however, if this action would be necessary, because the stockholders or subordinated debenture holders would have insisted that the bank be merged with another firm or be liquidated, rather than permit a government takeover that would be likely to dissipate the remaining net assets. Indeed, except for situations such as a massive fraud or exceptionally large and sudden losses, it is unlikely that the authorities would have to take the steps prescribed for an "undercapitalized" bank. Thus, except for administrative and monitoring expenses, deposit insurance would be almost costless.

**Deposits Offered by Other Companies—Collateralization.** As computer technology advances, both in terms of what can be done and how much it costs to do it, it seems likely that deposit-like fund-transfer services will be offered by companies not chartered as banks. If there were no chance that legislators would bail out holders of these accounts should the companies fail, there would be no externality and no justification for regulation. Based on experience, however, it is likely that these "depositors" would claim that they believed their accounts were insured and, if there were enough of them, their claims would be honored. Experience also indicates that if such a company appears to be close to failure, government officials will announce that there is nothing to worry about. After this point, a taxpayer bailout is very likely to occur when the holders of deposit-like accounts claim that they relied on the assurances of government officials. Examples of this phenomenon include the failure of an Australian thrift. When it failed, the presumably uninsured depositors, assured by state officials who had feared a run that their funds were safe, were bailed out by the taxpayers (Kane and Kaufman 1993). Another example is the taxpayer bailout of depositors in state-chartered credit unions and savings and loan associations who were not protected when privately run, state-chartered insurance funds in Rhode Island and Ohio became bankrupt. Perhaps the most costly (to taxpayers) example is the assumption by the Treasury of the obligations of the bankrupt Federal Savings and Loan Insurance Corporation (FSLIC).

The contingent taxpayer liability for deposit-like accounts with nonbanks can be removed by requiring companies offering this service to hold collateral that is sufficient to cover the "deposit" balances, net of conservatively estimated potential declines in the value of the collateral. The nonbanks would also be required to report the deposit balances and collateral values monthly to the authorities, subject to audit by independent public accountants. The companies would additionally be subject to a SEIR system of discretionary and mandatory intervention by the authorities, similar to that employed for banks.

Depository institutions might also choose collateralization as an alternative to capital requirements.[52]

## Government-Mandated Third-Party Liability Insurance, Life Insurance, and Annuities

These financial services are discussed together because they are all offered by insurance companies, for which the same optimal form of regulation applies. As is the situation for depositories, the stockholders of corporations that offer these products have incentives to take excessive risks and to dissipate resources, if they have relatively little of their own capital at stake and if their creditors have no reason to be or cannot be concerned about these actions. Although the insurance companies' liabilities are not government insured (as discussed in chapter 2), their third-party claimants cannot monitor and charge for the risks (as can creditors generally), and life insurance and annuity purchasers hold long-term contracts over which they have limited control. The solution is to establish and enforce capital requirements similar to those proposed for banks.

It is also important that insurance companies estimate their liabilities to policyholders and hold sufficient assets to meet those liabilities. As is now the situation, these determinations should be made by actuaries, and the companies' annual financial statements should be audited and attested to by independent public accountants.[53]

**Risk-Adjusted Capital and Deposit Insurance Premiums.** Almost as long as government-sponsored deposit insurance has been available, economists have pointed out that charging premiums that undercharge for risk could give rise to a moral hazard. Presumably, if banks or insurance companies were charged the same amount per dollar of deposits, regardless of the risks posed by the asset and liability holdings, they would tend to take greater risks. Nevertheless, risk-adjusted insurance premiums have never been applied by any country, with the recent exception of the United States for banks, as mandated by law in 1991. Even then, only slightly higher premiums were assessed against very few banks.

*Risk-weighting procedures.* Rather, the United States and other countries have attempted to control excessive risk taking by banks and insurance companies with supervisory monitoring and interventions and by limiting the assets in which they are permitted to invest to those believed to be prudent or relatively safe. Determining that the restrictions have not been subverted is a costly procedure, usually requiring field examinations. More costly still is the tendency of naturally conservative supervisors to disapprove of or disallow innovations that appear to be risky or that they do not understand. Furthermore, in practice, these restrictions have more often been employed to thwart competition that, perhaps inadvertently, has served to increase risk when the restrictions prevented banks from effectively diversifying their assets, liabilities, and operations.

At the same time, banks have not been prevented from engaging in very risky activities. For example, banks can make loans that have a high probability of defaulting. If they want to avoid recording high nominal interest rates, they can take payment in fees and up-front points or by having borrowers maintain noninterest-bearing demand deposits. Long-term, fixed-interest government bonds can be held, even though they are subject to considerable interest-rate risk. Derivative instruments that offer the possibility of both high gains and losses might be held as investments rather than as hedges. Although banking supervisors generally disapprove of deliberate risk taking, it is difficult for them to monitor and constrain all the forms that risk taking might take, particularly because the most risky asset—commercial loans—is the "heart" of banking. Indeed, most bank failures not attributable to fraud and self-dealing have been the result of loan-default losses and losses resulting from unexpected interest-rate changes (Benston 1991).

In addition, it is very difficult to construct a risk-based capital requirement that is more than crudely meaningful and that might not give rise to politically motivated rewards and penalties designed to allocate credit. The Basel (Bank for International Settlements) bank capital standard, which has been adopted by almost all developed countries, specifies only four classes of credit risk. Consequently, all commercial loans are considered to be equally risky, whether made to a major company with relatively low levels of debt or to a high-risk start-up enterprise. All home mortgage loans are given a 50 percent weighting, including those that are guaranteed by a government agency. But if those same mortgages are put into mortgage-backed bonds that are guaranteed by a government agency, the securities are assigned a 20 percent weight. Loans to all banks in the European Union are treated as equally risky. Furthermore, the risk weighting ignores the well-known fact that portfolios of assets and liabilities are almost always less risky than the sum of the risks of individual assets and liabilities, because total risk also depends on the covariances of the cash flows among the assets and liabilities. Indeed, the *portfolio* risk is the only relevant metric.[54]

Bank- or regulator-designed statistical models that purport to measure value at risk (VAR) have been suggested as a means of establishing the risks to which banks are exposed. But these models suffer from some serious shortcomings. For example, Goodhart et al. (1998, chapter 5) describe the three basic models and conclude that they can lead to substantially different risk estimates, depending on reasonable variations in the basic inputs to the models. Consequently, as long as bankers have incentives to understate their capital requirements, they can readily adjust the models to indicate a lower level of risk. To overcome such opportunistic gaming, the authorities might impose a substantial fine on a bank should it, ex post, have underpredicted a loss, as suggested by Paul Kupiec and James O'Brien (1995). There is reason to doubt, however, that this threat is credible: would the authorities really impose a heavy fine on a bank that has just incurred a large loss, thereby worsening its capital position?

The National Association of Insurance Commissioners (NAIC) has designed a risk-based capital formula and model law for life-health and property-liability companies, effective from 1993 and 1994. The formula encompasses four major risk categories—asset risk, credit risk, underwriting risk, and growth and off-balance-sheet risk. Different weights are applied to each group and to subgroups within the categories (for instance, underwriting risk includes loss expenses, reserves, and net premiums written for each line of business). The sum of the risk-based capital calculated for each "risk" is reduced through a covariance adjustment that is designed to reflect the effects of diversification.[55] No adjustment is made for interest-rate risk or for company size, even though most of the insolvencies appear to be of smaller companies (Cummins et al. 1995, table 3), probably because the larger companies are more diversified. This risk-based capital calculation appears to be better than that designed for banks; as Cummins et al. show, however, it is inadequate, in part because the risk weights are far from optimal.

*The suggested capital requirement.* The suggested capital requirement is not risk-weighted, for two related reasons and an overarching one. First, an economically satisfactory scheme for determining the optimal or even reasonably good weights has not been devised. On the contrary, the procedures recently adopted for banks and insurance companies suffer from serious shortcomings. Some of these are the result of political compromise, wherein low weights are applied to assets that are favored by politically powerful groups. Home mortgages and EU banks are two examples. Some shortcomings are attributable to the inherent difficulty of determining the risk weights the marketplace assigns to specific assets and liabilities. The attempt to obtain reliable numbers would be excessively costly to the regulated firms and to the regulators. Even if banks and insurance companies were willing to bear these costs, there are insufficient data to measure past risks with much precision, to say nothing of estimating the relevant expected risks. Additionally, the risk of insolvency is not the aggregate of the separately measured risks of assets and liabilities but rather their combination in a portfolio that takes into account the covariance of net cash flows from individual or groups of assets and liabilities. But it is unclear how to make the measurements unambiguously.

The second reason that risk weighting of capital is not recommended is this: should the level of capital be insufficient to cover almost all losses that a bank or insurance company might incur, the owners of these corporations would have incentives to "game" the system within the risk classifications. This would be costly, both in losses that might be imposed on the insurance fund or taxpayers, and in the misallocation of resources from modifications of operations made simply to reduce required capital. For example, mortgage-backed securities of government agency–guaranteed mortgages are accorded a 20 percent weight, although the same mortgages held individually by a bank would be given a 50 percent weight. Consequently, some banks might be willing to incur the expense of securitizing mortgages, selling the securities, and purchasing similar securities simply to reduce their capital requirements.

The overarching reason for not risk weighting capital is that with a sufficiently high capital-to-assets ratio, subordinated debt included fully as capital, and structured early intervention and resolution, few if any depositories or insurance companies will become insolvent. In addition, the interest paid on subordinated debentures serves as a risk-adjusted deposit insurance premium. Hence, the complications and inadequacies of a risk-based capital requirement need not be of concern.

## International Harmonization of National Regulations and Cooperation among Regulators

As international trade and transactions have increased, so too has international banking.[56] This development and its likely continuation and growth have raised four concerns, for which regulators have proposed harmonization of banking and securities regulations among countries and coordination among national bank and securities regulators as remedies. Their concerns are as follows:

1. Internationally organized banks will be able to avoid or evade national prudential regulations. The Bank for Credit and Commerce International (BCCI) is usually given as the prime example.

2. Without international harmonization, international banks will not be competing on a level playing field.

3. Payment-system risks cannot be contained without international harmonization of regulations.

4. Contagion is a serious problem—the failure of banks or stock market crashes in one country might cause a collapse in other countries.

As the following analysis shows, these concerns either are not really problems or are problems that would be dealt with effectively by the proposed capital regulation. But cooperation among national regulators could be beneficial.

**Avoidance or Evasion of National Prudential Regulations by Internationally Organized Banks.** Subsidiaries of foreign-chartered banks are simply domestic banks that have foreign owners. The capital requirements outlined at the beginning of this chapter would apply to all domestically chartered banks, including subsidiaries of banks chartered by other countries (hereinafter, foreign banks). Hence, this vital regulation could not be evaded.

Following the collapse of the Bank for Credit and Commerce International, the banking authorities have reason for concern that a foreign-chartered bank with subsidiaries in many countries might rapidly shift funds out of a domestic country that has stringent capital requirements. This concern, however, should apply to domestically owned as well as to foreign-owned banks. For either set of banks, the authorities should pay close attention to banks with controlling owners or owners or managers of questionable probity.

Branches of foreign banks could pose a domestic problem if the capital requirements of their home countries were inadequate. In this event, the national banking authorities could impose collateral requirements on the foreign-bank branches. This requirement would deal effectively with the situation where domestic depositors believed that all deposits were government-insured, but where a foreign country did not offer credible deposit insurance. Under the proposed system, there would be no other prudential regulations for a foreign bank to avoid or evade.

**Competition on a Level Playing Field.** As is explained earlier in this chapter, the proposed capital regulation is almost costless to banks. They would not be at a competitive disadvantage with respect to similarly regulated foreign banks. But an inadequately capitalized foreign bank is supported with a subsidy in the form of a contingent liability assumed by its country's de jure or de facto deposit insurance. Its country's taxpayers or domestic users of the bank's services, though, pay for the foreign bank's advantage. This is similar to government subsidies for any export. To the extent that a subsidized foreign bank would be in a position to out-compete domestic banks, people in the foreign bank's country would be transferring their wealth to the residents of the host country. From the perspective of consumers of the bank's services, this is a desirable outcome.

**Payment-System Risk.** The collapse of any bank, domestic or foreign, that participates in a payment system would be disruptive. But this problem can be dealt with effectively by an adequate capital requirement and settlement procedure. Banks chartered in countries that do not have such a capital requirement should be required to clear only in "good" funds or to collateralize their transactions, either directly or by having other adequately capitalized banks guarantee their payments. Cooperation among national regulators could, however, be useful if it resulted in the development of consistent or at least well-understood rules of law that applied to all cross-border, interbank transactions.

**Contagion.** As long as the money supply of a country is controlled by its own central bank, there cannot be a contagious run on either domestic or foreign banks that disrupts that country's financial system, as is explained in chapter 2. With respect to stock market contagion, as noted there, a rapid decline in stock prices in a foreign country might cause a domestic stock-price crash, if investors take the foreign crash as an indication that their domestic stocks are overvalued. This is not a situation that can be dealt with by regulating securities firms or transactions.

Alternatively, prices on a foreign stock market could have crashed because of a scandal that regulators might have been able to prevent. It is possible that domestic investors take this as a signal that a similar scandal could occur on the domestic market; they panic, and the domestic market crashes. First, this form of contagion is unlikely to occur. Second, even if it did happen, a negative externality would not result—there would simply be a transfer of wealth among investors. Hence, there is no justification for government regulation.

**Cooperation among National Regulators.** Cooperation with the regulatory authorities in foreign countries, including sharing of supervisory reports, could be useful for evaluating and monitoring the probity and financial conditions of foreign-based parent companies. When large-scale fraud is suspected, examination reports could be shared and joint examinations undertaken. Cooperation among regulators could also serve to reduce potential fraud and tax evasion.

Standardized reporting of financial data could be useful in reducing the information costs of national authorities and investors. But the development of such standards depends first on the existence of a set of data and a format for its presentation that most experienced observers would agree is optimal or, at least, acceptable. This agreement is difficult to achieve. Unlike the situation in the natural sciences (which also suffers from limitations), the methods and opportunities for determining what is "best" are not often present in financial economics. An additional complication is that people in different countries often honestly believe that the procedures followed by their countries dominate those used in other countries. This makes agreement on what is best or acceptable even more difficult to achieve.

In addition, individual countries and even individual regulatory bodies within countries emphasize their own agendas, which include their understanding of their missions, the interests of their bureaucracies and constituents, and the beliefs and prejudices of their leaders. Consequently, they argue for their own rules and regulations and reject those emphasized by others.

When they do agree (after many meetings over many years), it is often for a minimum set of rules, which actually may be less costly than the alternative of comprehensive rules. For example, the Basel Committee met for years before agreeing to the international risk-adjusted bank-capital standards that are based on very broad categories of credit risk and do not include consideration of portfolio risk and interest-rate risk. The International Organization of Securities Commissioners and Organizations (IOSCO) has been attempting for years to adopt a uniform set of minimum accounting disclosure standards. Agreement has been difficult, largely because the United States has insisted that its definition of "generally acceptable accounting principles" (GAAP) is the only acceptable one. The SEC has not been willing to permit U.S. investors to choose among securities of companies that offer different degrees or kinds of financial accounting disclosure, particularly foreign companies that follow GAAP defined by their home countries, even though U.S. investors could reject or discount the securities of those companies.

Harmonization of regulations among countries is much more difficult to attain than is cooperation among regulators, which is fortunate because harmonization is neither necessary nor useful for solving or mitigating banking and securities problems. As has already been discussed extensively, the consumers and taxpayers of a country benefit when financial-services providers and markets are not specially regulated, except with respect to capital for depositories and insurance companies. If other countries choose to regulate more extensively or intrusively, the cost is borne by their consumers and taxpayers. Importation of these regulations via harmonization with the more extensive regulations imposed by a more "enlightened" country would be detrimental to consumers in a country that adopted the system proposed here.

## Consumer Protection from Fraud, Unfair Dealing, and Invidious Discrimination

As is discussed in chapter 2, consumer protection has been an important reason for governmental regulation of financial-services providers. This goal, though, is ill met when agencies that are also charged with supervising those providers are given this responsibility. The argument for separating consumer protection from financial regulation is given next, followed by a proposal for an ombudsman agency that, I believe, would be more likely to serve consumers' interests.

**Separation of Consumer Protection from Financial Regulation.** Including consumer protection as a responsibility of a regulatory agency tends to be detrimental to consumers generally. The primary concern of financial-services regulatory agencies has been for the solvency and well-being of the institutions they supervise. Consequently, the regulators usually learn much about these firms and understand and identify with their problems. They may even view government service as a prelude to working for these firms. Senior regulators, in particular, are often in regular contact with the "best people" in the industry and come to see their view of how things should be done. They thus tend to have less sympathy with or understanding of the problems faced by consumers.

Regulators also involve industry representatives in the preparation and modification of regulation, to avoid imposing unnecessarily high costs on financial-services providers. As the document establishing the UK Financial Services Authority (paragraph 33) puts it, "It is important to continue to involve practitioners in the regulatory system." Larger, established, high-quality firms generally want to be involved and are likely to be asked to participate in the rule-setting process. These firms can afford the cost and have incentives to want their competitors to maintain the high standards they already follow.

As a result of the "natural" relationship between the regulators and the higher-quality regulated firms, consumers might be denied the opportunity of buying lower-cost (though lower-quality) products and services that might better suit their needs. Furthermore, "high standards" could be structured so as to discourage or prohibit the introduction of new products by maverick firms or industry outsiders that might threaten existing firms, with the explanation that the new products have terms that might mislead consumers or are difficult for the regulators to understand and monitor.

In contrast to "high-quality" industry people, individual consumers rarely have reason to contact regulatory agencies, because few consumers are defrauded, discriminated against, or dealt with unfairly. Of those who do contact an agency, some are confused or inarticulate, some are misinformed or poorly advised, and yet others are looking for an excuse to get out of a valid contract. Consequently, it is not surprising that the agencies tend not to cater to individual consumers. Indeed, because the regulators deal with existing chartered or licensed firms, they often overlook what they perceive to be "small-time" frauds perpetrated by con artists and fly-by-night firms. But these frauds impose great damage on relatively poor, less sophisticated, mentally impaired, and often infirm, lonely, and older people.

The often cozy relationship between the regulator and the regulated has changed somewhat over the past several decades, as some advocacy groups that purport to represent consumers have successfully publicized claims that financial-services firms have engaged in unfair and discriminatory practices. (More often than not, the claims have been shown to be invalid.) Currently, regulatory agencies such as the UK Financial Services Authority, its predecessors, and the many U.S. banking agencies are charged with protecting consumers. This "protection," however, at least in the United States, has often taken the form of following the dictates of advocacy groups.

**Ombudsman Agency.** Legislators might believe that they must actively "do something" to protect consumers from unfair treatment by financial-services providers. Or, they might believe that only government officials who specialize in financial products can effectively protect consumers. Given these assumptions, the best procedure would be to establish an independent agency to serve as an ombudsman for consumers who believe they have been mistreated by a financial-services firm or salesperson. These consumers could ask the agency to look into the situation. The agency could then either help them recover what they had lost or confirm that they had been fairly dealt with. If the agency found a particular practice to be objectionable, it could try to persuade industry participants to change, educate consumers, refer the matter to the legal authorities, or suggest legislative action.

As was explained in chapter 2, however, there is little justification for treating financial-products and -services producers differently from other producers. In practice, financial services are less subject to fraud, invidious discrimination, and unfair dealing than are many other products and services that are more important to the average consumer.

## Conclusions

The regulatory system described—high relative capital requirements, including subordinated debt, and structured early intervention and resolution imposed only on depositories and insurance companies—would be almost costless to taxpayers, the regulated companies, and consumers of their products and services. Inclusion of subordinated debt as capital would remove the income-tax cost of the capital requirement. Banks and insurance companies would then be free of regulation, other than the capital and reporting requirements (including attestation by independent public accountants and, for insurance companies, actuaries). These requirements would not constrain new entrants and new products. The cost of losses would and should pass to those who should bear them—the stockholders and subordinated debt holders of firms that offer insured deposits and some insurance products. Other banks and insurance companies (and possibly taxpayers) would have to pay only for the authorities' costs of monitoring and enforcing capital requirements, and for losses caused by massive frauds and extremely large defaults. They would also pay for reductions in the market value of securities that deplete some companies' capital before the authorities can act. But most losses would be avoided, because the proposed system of structured early intervention and resolution removes regulators' incentives to forbear from sanctioning and eventually closing weak institutions. The mandatory steps required under SEIR also remove the incentive of bankers to use political influence to delay regulatory intervention. Hence, bankers will either recapitalize, sell their banks, or liquidate rather than be taken over while their banks are still solvent.

An advantage of the proposed regulation is that risk need not be explicitly measured and included in the capital requirement for that requirement to be effective. A higher-than-at-present capital-to-assets ratio that is comparable to that of insured competitors would give owners of banks and insurance companies strong incentives to avoid excessive risks. Structured early intervention and resolution would provide for intervention and action by the authorities when an institution's capital is effectively depleted and this incentive is no longer strong. In addition, the interest rate paid by the institutions on subordinated debt imposes on them a market-determined risk charge or benefit. A higher rate and the difficulties experienced by banks and insurance companies in refinancing that debt also give the authorities early market-driven warnings of the institutions' solvency problems.

The considerable increase in international financial transactions should give domestic authorities little reason for concern. The capital requirement imposed on both domestic- and foreign-owned banks (as described above), along with the deposit collateral imposed on foreign-owned branches of companies headquartered in countries with insufficiently strong or effective capital requirements, should be sufficient to protect domestic deposits and insurance-company assets. Harmonization of regulations among countries is neither necessary nor desirable. But cooperation could be useful for evaluating questionable managers and owners, reducing fraud and tax evasion, and possibly reducing the authorities' and investors' information costs.

Consumer protection should not be a responsibility of the government agencies that are charged with monitoring and maintaining the solvency of banks and insurance companies. Consumers who might be subjected to fraud, unfair dealing, and invidious discrimination might be helped by a special purpose agency that acts as an ombudsman. However, these detrimental practices are less likely to be more prevalent among financial institutions and financial products than among many other firms and many other products. Hence, consumer protection should be general rather than specific in nature.

——————————— ⌘ ———————————

# *Notes*

1. See Benston (1983) for a more extensive review of U.S. regulation of financial-services firms, and Benston (1976) for an outline and comparison of financial accounting–disclosure rules in the United States and the United Kingdom.

2. Pension plans are not included, because they are part of the employment agreement; hence, they do not give rise to an externality.

3. I first examined this question in Benston (1972), refined the analysis in Benston (1983), and updated it in Benston (1987).

Additional analysis and critique are presented in Benston (1995b). Justifications for regulation given by other commentators are less comprehensive.

In their extensive monograph, Goodhart et al. (1998) consider only three reasons for regulating financial institutions. As summarized in their chapter 9, these are: "to preserve the financial system from systematic and contagious instability"; "a need for continuous monitoring of the behaviour of financial firms [because] many [financial] contracts are long term in nature and involve a fiduciary responsibility"; and "to protect the consumer . . . [by] correcting identified market imperfections and failures." I consider these and other reasons in chapter 2 of this book. In their chapters 4 and 5, Goodhart et al. also cogently point out the reasons for and costs and limitations of regulation, which I consider in chapter 3 of this book.

Kane (1997, 54) offers three "standard [which he calls 'altruistic'] justifications for government regulation of deposit institutions. . . . First, a particular society's welfare can be served by directing financial institutions to alter the distribution of wealth by offering socially deserving parties free or subsidized access to selected . . . services." He dismisses this justification (as do I) because "deadweight losses make it hard to engineer advantaged access to financial-institution services in ways that either compensate efficiently for whatever disadvantages face the class of intended beneficiaries or efficiently reward the beneficiaries' extraordinary social 'worthiness.' . . . Second, monopoly power and externalities that might emerge in producing and delivering financial services may be cited as justifications. . . . Authorities mention three efficiency goals: to save resources by coordinating institutional activity; to prevent industry monopolization; and to minimize the chance of contagious consumer runs." I consider the first below in the text. The second, monopolization, is dismissed by Kane, Goodhart, et al. and by me; we all argue that reduced restrictions on entry and existing antitrust statutes would deal with this problem effectively, to the extent that it is a problem. Kane concludes: "In practice, the authorities emphasize the third goal: to block 'systemic' (i.e., economy-wide) damage from a cascade of financial-institution failures." This is considered below in the text.

In Benston (1994b, section 3) I also examine and find that regulation of banks is not necessary for the government to conduct or enhance monetary (macroeconomic) policy. In section 4 of that article I analyze government allocation of credit and control of capital as justifications for bank regulation, and find that these purposes are not desirable from a public-interest perspective. Nor would bank regulation render them effective, particularly for countries such as the United States and the United Kingdom.

4. The Chinese used paper money, called "flying money," long before other people, because they had a strong central government run by able bureaucrats who could be relied on to limit the supply of paper money—much as central banks in modern times usually do, with some notable exceptions.

5. The two exceptions to this practice were the unrenewed twenty-year charters of the First and Second Banks of the United States.

6. As a consequence of inflation and a progressive income tax, more taxpayers pay higher taxes, because their higher nominal incomes are taxed at higher rates. The nominally determined tax brackets are not raised to account for the reduced purchasing power of money.

7. Conceptually, a single bank could exist as a result of economies of scale. But a substantial amount of empirical research (beginning with Benston 1965) for small commercial banks, for savings and loan associations (Benston 1970), and for large banks (Benston, Hanweck, and Humphrey 1982), plus many excellent studies by other researchers,

finds little evidence of substantial economies of scale. Furthermore, there are no examples of a single bank dominating a market that is not constrained by restrictions on entry.

8. This is explained more fully by Calomiris and Kahn (1991).

9. See Benston (1994a) for citations to and a review of this evidence.

10. From 1934 through 1982, the FDIC paid off deposits of $1,085 million in 319 generally small banks, and it assisted in the assumption of the $18,873 million in deposits in 301 banks. See Golembe and Holland (1983, 51).

11. See Benston (1995a) for a more extensive discussion and citations to other studies.

12. The Federal Deposit Insurance Corporation Improvement Act of 1991 (FDICIA) requires very senior government officials (including the president) to approve the bailout of uninsured depositors; however, this provision of the law has not yet been tested.

13. Edward Kane has emphasized these agency costs in his many writings—for example, Kane (1997).

14. In Benston (1997b) I delineate the information required for specific kinds of financial instruments and explain in detail the virtual impossibility for a government agency to prespecify the required information.

15. See Benston (1981) for a description of the laws, the situation that led to their enactment, and a review and critique of redlining studies.

16. Actually, there is no empirical support for the assumption of underserved markets in the United States; see Benston and Horsky (1991) for research on redlining that accounts for unmet demand as well as the supply of mortgages; Yezer (1995) for a compendium of articles on redlining; and Benston, Hunter, and Kaufman (1997) for more recent papers.

17. "Protection" of consumers from having to pay "high" prices or get "poor quality" products or service is discussed in chapter 4.

18. See Benston and Kaufman (1996) for additional arguments rebutting Dow's rationale for regulating banks.

19. See White (1984, 26).

20. The term *Blue Sky* comes from a description of the first of such laws, which was enacted by the state of Kansas in 1911. These laws were so named because stock promoters were said to be selling "building lots in the blue sky in fee simple." (Mofsky 1971, 10.)

21. Benston (1976 and 1997a).

22. They are the Building Societies Commission, Friendly Societies Commission, Insurance Directorate of the Department of Trade and Industry, Investment Management Regulatory Organization, Personal

Investment Authority, Registry of Friendly Societies, Securities and Futures Authority, Securities and Investments Board, and the Supervision and Surveillance Division of the Bank of England.

23. Unless otherwise specified, the quotations are from page 1 of the document.

24. The Report to the Chancellor (1997) does not include a discussion of the reasons for the specified "high-level aims" of the FSA.

25. See Benston (1997a, 8–10) for a more extensive discussion and illustration of the information people might want to evaluate specific financial products.

26. See Benston and Kaufman (1995) for a review of and citations to the evidence from which this conclusion is drawn.

27. As is discussed later, banks did not oppose much of this legislation, because it benefited them by limiting competition.

28. A very large body of empirical research could be cited. See for example Benston (1977) for a study of the negative impact on consumers of the imposition of U.S. state-imposed rate ceilings on consumer loans, and Harrington (1984) and Meier (1988, 156–59), who find that price regulation by U.S. state insurance commissions has no impact on the price of insurance.

29. See Benston (1997a), however, for an analysis of the inherent difficulty for a government agency to specify disclosure that would be useful to the purchasers of financial products, and for the argument that voluntary disclosure, not mandated disclosure, is the preferable alternative to government vetting of financial instruments and services.

30. Kane (1997, 54) mentions an "efficiency goal" justification for regulation: "to save resources by coordinating institutional activity"; but he does not elaborate further.

31. For a critique of mandated financial accounting disclosure, see Benston (1969, 1975b, and 1976).

32. Durkin and Elliehausen (1990, 258).

33. Benston (1969, 66–69). The measure used is the ratio of net equity issues to gross and net (of depreciation, adjusted for changes in replacement costs) capital expenditures of U.S. manufacturing and mining corporations between 1900 and 1953, the last year for which these data are available. The data show that after passage of the Securities Act of 1933 net equity issues were negative (redemptions exceeded new issues) until 1938. There were no other changes in exogenous reasons for firms to substitute debt for equity (such as a change in the income tax provisions).

34. Curiously, as Klein (1995, 385, n.19) reports: "The NAIC model act prohibits insurers, agents, and other parties from using an insurer's RBC [risk-based capital] results in marketing efforts."

35. See Benston (1991) for a review of empirical studies from which this conclusion is drawn.

36. A more complete description of these developments may be found in Benston (1984).

37. Goodhart (1988) similarly delineates the cost of regulation with respect to the UK Financial Services Act.

38. They also report data on the regulatory agencies' costs related to life insurance and personal and financial advice.

39. Additional discussion and evidence is presented in Benston (1991).

40. Direct investments in real estate by S&Ls, however, did not contribute substantially to the losses, but rather tended to mitigate them, as shown in Benston (1989).

41. See Benston and Carhill (1994) for an analysis of the savings and loan disaster based on a restatement of S&Ls' financial statements to market values over the period from 1984 through 1988.

42. Meier (1985) describes, criticizes, and integrates theories of regulation that include political and sociological explanations, as well as economic explanations (which he finds inadequate). Also see Benston (1976 chapter 5) for an application of the wider theory to the regulation of financial disclosure by the SEC compared with regulation then employed in the United Kingdom.

43. Probably the best known expositions of the "capture" theory, which suggests that regulation is enacted and extended to meet the demands of regulated firms, are Stigler (1971), Peltzman (1976), and Posner (1974).

44. See Benston and Kaufman (1994) for a comparison of the proposed system and FDICIA, and Benston and Kaufman (1997) for an assessment of the act after five years. (So far, so good!)

45. See Benston (1992) for an analysis of the benefits and measurement of capital for depository institutions.

46. Kaufman (1992) presents capital/asset ratios for commercial banks and for several industries in the United States. These numbers show that before deposit insurance was enacted in 1933, on average the ratio for commercial banks was about 15 percent. At that time, however, banks were subject to supervision, which limited the risks they might take, and to fast closure as a result of actual or prospective deposit runs. For the finance industry as a whole, the ratio in 1986 was 18.8 percent. Other industries have considerably higher ratios. Benink and Benston (1999) measure the capital/asset ratios of banks in European Union countries in the late nineteenth and in the twentieth centuries, and find that they decline from more than 25 percent through the late nineteenth century to about 15 percent from 1910 to 1934.

There is strong evidence that the currently imposed ratios are too low. Jones and King (1995, 491) find that "from 1984 through 1989, the vast majority of banks exhibiting a high risk of insolvency would not have been considered undercapitalized based on the current risk-based capital (RBC) standards, and so would not have been subject to mandatory corrective actions under FDICIA." Cummins, Harrington, and Klein (1995, 526) report similar findings for insurance companies: "fewer than half of the companies that later failed had RBC ratios within the proposed ranges for regulatory and company action."

47. See Benston (1997c) for an analysis of accounting for derivatives used as hedges.

48. This analysis is taken largely from Benston (1998).

49. A related person would be defined as a close relative and a related firm might be one in which these people have an interest greater than their proportionate holding of the bank's capital.

50. Some observers might be concerned that because CPAs are engaged by banks, they might not in practice be independent and reliable auditors and reporters of their clients' financial statements and affairs. But as I analyze in some detail in Benston (1985), CPAs have substantial investments in their reputations for both integrity and expertise. Their economic well-being would be seriously damaged if they were suborned by their clients or were ineffective auditors. Although there are some instances in which CPAs have conducted sloppy, even incompetent, audits, there are almost no recorded cases of CPAs deliberately attesting to false or misleading financial statements. Notably, some CPA firms in the United States have been charged with conducting poor audits of some savings and loan associations. The fact that S&Ls were required to be audited by CPAs, however, probably reduced the amount of losses they imposed on taxpayers, considering that the Federal Home Loan Bank Board permitted economically insolvent S&Ls to remain open. One also must consider the acknowledged understaffing of its examination and supervision staff as a result of the Reagan administration's downsizing of federal regulatory agencies.

51. In his many writings, Edward Kane emphasizes and elaborates on the perverse (from the viewpoint of taxpayers) incentives faced by regulators and the means they take to avoid being held accountable for not acting promptly and effectively. See Kane (1997) for a recent exposition that is cited, at length, in Goodhart et al. (1998, chapter 4).

52. See Benston et al. (1989) for a more complete discussion of this alternative. Also, see Benston et al. (1989) and Benston and Kaufman (1988, 42–43) for analysis and rejection of the "narrow bank" or "fail safe" proposal, wherein depositories would be required to invest only in short-term government obligations, or their equivalent.

53. The National Association of Insurance Commissioners also subjects to statistical analysis a large amount of data reported by insurance companies. In addition, it conducts field examinations based on this analysis. Whether this additional level of supervision is cost effective has not been examined, to my knowledge.

54. See Benston (1992) for a detailed description and critique of the Basle risk-based capital standard.

55. See Cummins et al. (1995) for more details and references.

56. This section is derived from Benston (1994b), which includes a more comprehensive analysis and references to other studies.

# References

Benink, Harald A., and George J. Benston. 1999. "The Future of Banking Regulation in Developed Countries: Lessons from and for Europe." Unpublished paper, Emory University (United States) and Maastricht University (Netherlands).

Benston, George J. 1964. "Interest Payments on Demand Deposits and Bank Investment Behavior." *Journal of Political Economy* 62 (October): 431–49.

———. 1965. "Economies of Scale and Marginal Costs in Banking Operations." *National Banking Review* 2 (June): 507–49.

———. 1969. "The Effect and Effectiveness of the SEC's Accounting Disclosure Requirements." Pp. 23–79 in *Economic Policy and the Regulation of Corporate Securities*, ed. Henry G. Manne. Washington, D.C.: AEI Press.

———. 1970. "Cost of Operations and Economies of Scale in Savings and Loan Associations." Pp. 677–761 in *Study of the Savings and Loan Industry*, ed. Irwin Friend. Washington, D.C.: Federal Home Loan Bank Board, U.S. Government Printing Office.

———. 1972. "The Optimal Banking Structure: Theory and Evidence from the United States." *Kredit und Kapital* 5 (December): 438–76. Also published in the *Journal of Bank Research* 3 (Winter) 1973: 220–36.

———. 1973a. "Required Disclosure and the Stock Markets: An

Evaluation of the Securities Exchange Act of 1934." *American Economic Review* 63 (March): 132–55.

———. 1973b. *Bank Examination*. Bulletins 89–90. Salomon Brothers Center for the Study of Financial Institutions, New York University Graduate School of Business Administration, May.

———. 1975a. "Accounting Standards in the U.S. and the U.K.: Their Nature, Causes and Consequences." *Vanderbilt Law Review* 28 (January): 235–68.

———. 1975b. "A Critique of the Rationale for Required Corporate Financial Disclosure." In *Emanuel Saxe Distinguished Lecture Series, 1973–74*, ed. Reed K. Storey. New York: Baruch College of the City University of New York.

———. 1976. *Corporate Financial Disclosure in the U.K. and the U.S.A.* London: Institute of Chartered Accountants in England and Wales, and New York: D.C. Heath.

———. 1977. "The Impact of Maturity Regulation on High Interest Rate Lenders and Borrowers." *Journal of Financial Economics* 4 (January): 23–49.

———. 1979. *Investors' Use of Financial Accounting Statement Numbers: A Review of Evidence from Stock Market Research*. Glasgow: University of Glasgow Press.

———. 1981. "Mortgage Redlining Research: A Review and Critical Analysis." *Journal of Bank Research* 12 (Spring): 8–23. A longer version appears in the Federal Reserve Bank of Boston, *Conference Series* 21 (October 1979): 144–95.

———. 1983. "Federal Regulation of Banking: Analysis and Policy Recommendations." *Journal of Bank Research* 13 (Winter): 216–44.

———. 1984. "Interest on Deposits and the Survival of Chartered Depository Institutions." *Economic Review*, Federal Reserve Bank of Atlanta, (October): 42–56.

———. 1985. "The Market for Public Accounting Services: Demand, Supply and Regulation." *Journal of Accounting and Public Policy* 4 (Spring): 33–79. A slightly different, earlier version was published in 1979–1980 in *The Accounting Journal* 4: 1–46.

———. 1987. "Why Continue to Regulate Banks? A Historical Assessment of Federal Banking Regulation." *Midland Corporate Finance Journal* 5 (Fall): 67–82.

———. 1989. "Direct Investments and FSLIC Losses." Pp. 25–77

in *Research in Financial Services: Private and Public Policies,* ed. George G. Kaufman. Greenwich, Conn.: JAI Press.

————. 1990. *The Separation of Commercial and Investment Banking: The Glass-Steagall Act Revisted and Reconsidered.* London: Macmillan Press, Ltd., and New York: Oxford University Press.

————. 1991. "Does Bank Regulation Produce Stability? Lessons from the United States." Pp. 207–32 in *Unregulated Banking: Order or Chaos?* ed. Forest Capie and Geoffrey E. Wood. London: Macmillan Press, Ltd..

————. 1992. "The Purpose of Capital for Institutions with Government-Insured Deposits." *Journal of Financial Services Research* 5: 369–84.

————. 1994a. "Market Discipline: The Role of Uninsured Depositors and Other Market Participants." Pp. 65–95 in *Safeguarding the Banking System in an Environment of Financial Cycles,* ed. Richard E. Randall, Federal Reserve Bank of Boston Conference Series no. 37.

————. 1994b. "International Harmonization of Banking Regulations and Cooperation among National Regulators: An Assessment." *Journal of Financial Services Research* 8: 205–25.

————. 1995a. "Safety Nets and Moral Hazard in Banking." Pp. 320–77 in *Financial Stability in a Changing Environment,* ed. Kuniho Sawamoto, Zenata Nakajima, and Hiroo Taguchi. New York: St. Martin's Press.

————. 1995b. "The Sins of Banking in the USA." *Economic Affairs* 15 (Spring): 18–23.

————. 1997a. *Voluntary vs. Mandated Disclosure.* Wellington, N.Z.: New Zealand Business Roundtable.

————. 1997b. "Discrimination in Mortgage Lending: Why HMDA and CRA Should be Repealed." *Journal of Retail Banking Services* 19 (Autumn): 47–57.

————. 1997c. "Accounting for Derivatives: Back to Basics." *Journal of Applied Corporate Finance* 10 (Fall): 46–58.

————. 1998. "Entry and Exit of Banks in Latin America and the Caribbean: Public Policy Concerns and a Proposed Solution." Published in Spanish as *Ingreso y Retiro de Bancos en América Latina y el Caribe: Preocupaciones por la Política Pública y Propuesta de una Solución.* Superbancaria, Superintendencia Bancaria de Colombia, Revista 33 (Marzo): 25–36.

Benston, George J., R. Dan Brumbaugh, Jr., Jack M. Guttentag,

Richard J. Herring, George G. Kaufman, Robert E. Litan, and Kenneth E. Scott. 1989. *Reconstructing America's Financial Institutions*. Washington, D.C.: Brookings Institution.

Benston, George J., and Mike Carhill. 1994. "The Causes and Consequences of the Thrift Disaster." In *Research in Financial Services*, ed. George G. Kaufman, 103–69. Greenwich, Conn.: JAI Press.

Benston, George J., Robert A. Eisenbeis, Paul M. Horvitz, Edward J. Kane, and George G. Kaufman. 1986. *Perspectives on Safe and Sound Banking: Past, Present, and Future*. Cambridge, Mass.: MIT Press.

Benston, George J., Gerald A. Hanweck, and David B. Humphrey. 1982. "Scale Economies in Banking: A Restructuring and Reassessment." *Journal of Money, Credit and Banking* 14 (November, part 1): 435–56.

Benston, George J., and Dan Horsky. 1991. "The Relationship between the Demand and Supply of Home Financing and Neighborhood Characteristics: An Empirical Study of Mortgage Redlining." *Journal of Financial Services Research* 10 (Summer): 72–87.

Benston, George J., Dan Horsky, and H. Martin Weingartner. 1978. *An Empirical Study of Mortgage Redlining*. Monograph Series in Finance and Economics, Salomon Brothers Center for the Study of Financial Institutions, New York University Graduate School of Business Administration, Monograph 1978–5.

Benston, George J., Curt Hunter, and George G. Kaufman, eds. 1997. *Discrimination in Financial Services*. Boston: Kluwer Academic Services.

Benston, George J., and George G. Kaufman. 1988. *Risk and Solvency Regulation of Depository Institutions: Past Policies and Current Options*. Monograph Series in Finance and Economics, Salomon Brothers Center for the Study of Financial Institutions, New York University Graduate School of Business Administration, Monograph 1988–1. A shorter version appears as "Regulating Bank Safety and Performance," in *Restructuring the Financial System*, ed. William S. Haraf and Rose Marie Kushmeider. Washington, D.C.: AEI Press, 1988.

———. 1990. "Understanding the Savings and Loan Debacle." *The Public Interest* 99 (Spring): 79–95.

———. 1994. "Improving the FDIC Improvement Act: What Was

Done and What Still Needs to Be Done to Fix the Deposit Insurance System." Pp. 99–120 in *Reforming Financial Institutions and Markets in the United States*, ed. George G. Kaufman. Boston: Kluwer Academic Publishers.

———. 1995. "Is the Banking and Payments System Fragile?" *Journal of Financial Services Research* 9: 209–40.

———. 1996. "The Appropriate Role of Bank Regulation." *Economic Journal* 106 (May): 688–97.

———. 1997. "FDICIA after Five Years." *Journal of Economic Perspectives* 11 (Summer): 139–58.

Bernard, Victor. 1989. "Capital Market Research in Accounting During the 1980s: A Critical Review." Pp. 72–120 in *Illinois Ph.D. Jubilee, 1939–1989: The State of Accounting Research as We Enter the 1990s*, ed. T. J. Frecka. Champaign-Urbana, Ill.: University of Illinois Press.

Calomiris, Charles W., and Charles M. Kahn. 1991. "The Role of Demandable Debt in Structuring Optimal Banking Arrangements." *American Economic Review* 81 (June): 497–513.

Calomiris, Charles W., and Joseph R. Mason. 1997. "Contagion and Bank Failures during the Great Depression: The June 1932 Chicago Bank Panic." *American Economic Review* 87: 863–83.

Cho, Jang Youn, and Kooyul Jung. 1991. "Earnings Response Coefficients: A Synthesis of Theory and Empirical Evidence." *Journal of Accounting Literature* 10: 87–116.

Coase, Ronald. 1960. "The Problem of Social Costs." *Journal of Law and Economics* 3: 1–44.

Cummins, J. David. 1988. "Risk-based Premiums for Insurance Guarantee Funds." *Journal of Finance* 43: 823–39.

Cummins, J. David, Scott E. Harrington, and Robert W. Klein. 1995. "Insolvency Experience, Risk-based Capital, and Prompt Corrective Action in Property-Liability Insurance." *Journal of Banking and Finance* 19 (June): 511–28.

Diamond, Douglas. 1984. "Financial Intermediation and Delegated Monitoring." *Review of Economic Studies* 51: 393–414.

Diamond, Douglas, and Philip Dybvig. 1983. "Bank Runs, Liquidity and Deposit Insurance." *Journal of Political Economy* 91: 401–19.

Dow, Sheila. 1996. "Why the Banking System Should Be Regulated." *Economic Journal* 106 (May): 698–707.

Downs, Anthony. 1967. *Inside Bureaucracy.* Boston: Little, Brown.

Durkin, Thomas A., and Gregory E. Elliehausen. 1990. "The Issue of Market Transparency: Truth-in-Lending Disclosure Requirements as Consumer Protections in the United States." In *Enhancing Consumer Choice*, Proceedings of the Second International Conference on Research in the Consumer Interest, ed. Robert M. Mayer, 255–65. Snowbird, Utah: American Council on Consumer Interests.

Franks, Julian R., Stephen M. Schaefer, and Michael D. Staunton. 1997. "The Direct and Compliance Costs of Financial Regulation." *Journal of Banking and Finance* 21: 1547–72.

Golembe, Carter H. 1975. "Memorandum Re: Interest on Demand Deposits." Washington, D.C.: Carter H. Golembe Associates, Inc.

Golembe, Carter H., and David S. Holland. 1983. *Federal Regulation of Banking 1983–84.* Washington, D.C.: Golembe Associates, Inc.

Gonedes, Nicholas J., and Nicholas Dopuch. 1974. "Capital Market Equilibrium, Information Production, and Selecting Accounting Techniques: Theoretical Framework and Review of Empirical Work." *Studies on Financial Accounting Objectives*, Supplement to *Journal of Accounting Research* 12: 48–129.

Goodhart, Charles. 1988. "The Costs of Regulation." Pp. 17–31 in *Financial Regulation—Or, Over-Regulation*, ed. A. Seldon. London: Institute of Economic Affairs.

Goodhart, Charles, Philipp Hartmann, David T. Llewellyn, Liliana Rojas-Suárez, and Steven R. Weisbrod. 1998. *Financial Regulation: Why, How and Where?* London: Routledge.

Harrington, Scott. 1984. "The Impact of Rate Regulation on Prices and Underwriting Results in the Property-Liability Insurance Industry: A Survey." *Journal of Risk and Insurance* 51 (December): 577–623.

Jarrell, Gregg A. 1981. "The Economic Effects of Federal Regulation of the Market for New Securities Issues." *Journal of Law and Economics* 24 (December): 613–75.

Jones, David, and Kathleen Kuester King. 1995. "The Implementation of Prompt Corrective Action: An Assessment." *Journal of Banking and Finance* 19: 491–510.

Kane, Edward J. 1997. "Ethical Foundations of Financial Regulation." *Journal of Financial Accounting Research* 12 (August): 51–74.

Kane, Edward J., and George G. Kaufman. 1993. "Incentive Conflict in Deposit Insurance Regulation: Evidence from Australia." *Pacific-Basin Finance Journal* 1: 13–29.

Kaufman, George G. 1992. "Capital in Banking: Past, Present and Future." *Journal of Financial Services Research* 5: 385–401.

———. 1994. "Bank Contagion: A Review of the Theory and Evidence." *Journal of Financial Services Research* 8, 123–50.

———. 1996. "Bank Failures, Systemic Risk, and Bank Regulation." *Cato Journal* 16 (Spring/Summer): 17–45.

Klein, Robert W. 1995. "Insurance Regulation in Transition." *Journal of Risk and Insurance* 62: 363–404.

Kupiec, Paul H., and James A. O'Brien. 1995. "A Pre-commitment Approach to Capital Requirements for Market Risk." Board of Governors, Federal Reserve System, Finance and Economics Discussion Series 95–36, July. Updated as "The Pre-commitment Approach: Using Incentives to Set Market Risk Capital Requirements," Board of Governors, Federal Reserve System, Finance and Economics Discussion Series 97–14, March 1997.

Llewellyn, David T. 1995. "Regulation of Retail Investment Services." *Economic Affairs* 15 (Spring): 12–17.

———. 1998. "Report on George Benston's Paper." Unpublished.

Lev, Baruch, and James A. Ohlson. 1982. "Market-based Empirical Research in Accounting: A Review, Interpretation, and Extension." *Journal of Accounting Research* Supplement 20: 249–322.

Meier, Kenneth J. 1985. *Regulation: Politics, Bureaucracy and Economics*. New York: St. Martin's Press.

———. 1988. *The Political Economy of Regulation: The Case of Insurance*. Albany, N.Y.: State University of New York Press.

Mofsky, James S. 1971. *Blue Sky Restrictions on New Business Promotions*. New York: Mathew Bender.

Peltzman, Sam. 1976. "Towards a More General Theory of Regulation." *Journal of Law and Economics* 19 (August): 211–40.

Posner, Richard A. 1974. "Theories of Economic Regulation." *Bell Journal of Economics and Management Science* 5 (Autumn): 337–52.

Report to the Chancellor. 1997. *On the Reform of the Financial Regulatory System*. London: Securities and Investment Board. July.

Rojas-Suárez, Liliana, and Steven R. Weisbrod. 1997. "Towards an Effective Financial Regulatory and Supervisory Framework for Latin America: Dealing with the Transition." In *Safe and Sound Financial Systems: What Works for Latin America,* ed. Liliana Rojas-Suárez, 35–74. Washington, D.C.: Inter-American Development Bank.

Schwartz, Anna. 1986. "Real and Pseudo-financial Crises." In *Financial Crises and the World Banking System*, ed. Forrest Capie and Geoffrey E. Wood, 11–31. London: Macmillan, Ltd.

Stigler, George J. 1971. "The Theory of Economic Regulation." *Bell Journal of Economics and Management Science* 2 (Spring): 3–21.

Tallman, Ellis, and Jon Moen. 1994. "Liquidity Shocks and Financial Crises during the National Banking Era." Unpublished manuscript, Federal Reserve Bank of Atlanta, April.

White, Lawrence H. 1984. *Free Banking in Britain: Theory, Experience, and Debate, 1800–1845.* Cambridge: Cambridge University Press.

Yezer, Anthony M., ed. 1995. *Fair Lending Analysis: A Compendium of Essays on the Use of Statistics.* Washington, D.C.: American Bankers Association.

# Index

# ✿ About the Author

George J. Benston is the John H. Harland Professor of Finance, Accounting, and Economics at the Goizueta Business School and professor of economics at the College of Arts and Sciences of Emory University, and honorary visiting professor at City University, London. Before coming to Emory in 1987, he was on the faculties of the University of Rochester and the University of Chicago, and he has been the John M. Olin Distinguished Visiting Fellow at Oxford University and a visiting professor at the London School of Economics, the London Graduate School of Business Studies, Hebrew University, and the University of California, Berkeley.

Professor Benston presently serves as coeditor of the *Journal of Financial Services Research*, and he is a member of the Shadow Financial Regulatory Committee and the Financial Economists' Roundtable. He has published more than one hundred books, monographs, and articles on banking and finance, accounting, and other aspects of economics. He received his Ph.D. from the University of Chicago, M.B.A. from New York University, and B.A. from Queens College.

A NOTE ON THE BOOK

*This book was edited by Cheryl Weissman*
*of the publications staff of the*
*American Enterprise Institute.*
*The index was prepared by Lee Brower.*
*The text was set in New Century Schoolbook.*
*Coghill Composition Company*
*of Richmond, Virginia, set the type, and*
*Edwards Brothers of Lillington, North Carolina,*
*printed and bound the book, using permanent*
*acid-free paper.*

The AEI PRESS is the publisher for the American Enterprise Institute for
Public Policy Research, 1150 17th Street, N.W., Washington, D.C. 20036;
*Christopher DeMuth,* publisher; *James Morris,* director; *Ann Petty,* editor;
*Leigh Tripoli,* editor; *Cheryl Weissman,* editor; *Kenneth Krattenmaker,* art
director and production manager; *Jean-Marie Navetta,* production assistant.

www.ingramcontent.com/pod-product-compliance
Lightning Source LLC
Jackson TN
JSHW011939131224
75386JS00041B/1458